BECKY SCOTT

THE WINNER WITHIN

A Special
Limited Edition
for *SUCCESS*
Subscribers

Also By Pat Riley

Show Time

Pat Riley

THE WINNER WITHIN

A Life Plan for Team Players

G. P. Putnam's Sons / New York

G. P. Putnam's Sons
Publishers Since 1838
200 Madison Avenue
New York, NY 10016

Book design: H. Roberts

Library of Congress Cataloging-in-Publication Data

Riley, Pat.
    The winner within : a life plan for team players / Pat Riley.
        p. cm.
    ISBN 0-399-13910-9 (alk. paper)
    1. Teamwork (Sports) 2. Work groups. 3. Cooperativeness.
    4. Interpersonal relations. I. Title.
    GV706.8.R54 1993   93-23770 CIP
    796'.01—dc20

Printed in the United States of America
1 2 3 4 5 6 7 8 9 10

This book is printed on acid-free paper.

DEDICATION

To my late father, Lee Riley. I want to dedicate this book to his voice and his presence. They have been with me since his death. I never got to say goodbye or to tell you I loved you. With this book I say hello, and thank you for inspiring me to:

> Plant my feet.
> Stand firm.
> And make a point
> about who I am.

> Your son, "Coach"

CONTENTS

ACKNOWLEDGMENTS

The first and most important team in anyone's life is their family. And, first of all that means Chris, twenty-three years my wife and my wife forevermore. In her life, it all started with innocence, but that innocence has blossomed into tremendous growth and insight. We have been partners in life and in developing the philosophies of this book. The writing of this book and the evolution of its ideas has definitely been a true team effort for the two of us.

As the writing went along, my young son James added the inspiration of his piano wizardry and his gifts as a budding songwriter, particularly with the lyrics to "Goodbye My Friend"—reprinted in this book with his permission, I might add. His little sister Elisabeth also helped remind me to stick with the basics of what I was trying to get across. "What's daddy *writing?* What's he *d-o-i-n-g?*" she kept asking. And, you know it helped keep me on track.

My Mom, Mary Riley, is 80 + and going strong. Her journey from innocence to personal growth started as she traveled with six kids in that old Woody station wagon, following my father from town to town in the coaching assignments that made up his career. And, she raised some wonderful brothers and sisters of mine in Lee, Mary Kay, Dennis, Elizabeth, and my late brother Lenny (who is survived by his lovely wife, Katie, and beautiful daughter, Kelly).

Chris's parents, Frank and Dorothy Rodstrom, have left their usual positive mark on anything important in our life. Frank brought his submarine to this book and Dorothy her Bible. As you'll see later: what a combination! And then there are Chris's four brothers: Tom, Bill, John, and Richard. And the rest of the Rodstrom and Riley clans.

Byron Laursen, whom I met in 1987 and who worked diligently with me on my first book, *Show Time,* was a crucial partner in getting this book written. Byron knew me, the Lakers, my voice, and my viewpoints. He gave me tremendous support, and his work in building the foundation of the book was absolutely essential. To him and his lovely wife, Theresa, who would get him up, fetch him the *Los Angeles Times,* send him on to the Village Cafe for an eye-opening coffee, and beckon him back to the computer and his work. Many thanks to a true Showtime Warrior.

As I mention Byron, I cannot forget to credit Rob Ryder, who assisted Byron with the research and assembled and verified a host of details.

I also want to thank Ron and Jan Beyma, who at the eleventh hour put a tremendous amount of time, effort, and business savvy into the final structure. And, they are the global teammates in this collaboration since they did it all from their workshop over in Europe.

So much of this book involves the players, coaches, and management of the teams I have been privileged to be a part. How could I not thank them . . . for the experiences as well as the wisdom that they have contributed to this book? I especially want to thank Jerry Buss, the owner of the Los Angeles Lakers, for the opportunity he gave me . . . and also longtime Lakers Jerry West, Chick Hearn, Bill Bertka, and Randy Pfund.

Then there is that close circle of what I like to think of as my "personal team"—with me on this effort as on every other:

Lisa Carroll, my administrator, who is a pure-bred team player and who understands the word loyalty in an unmatched way. Thank you for a great effort!

Steve and Holly Chabre. Best friends. Always friends. Right there with inspiration and support.

Ed Hookstratten and his remarkable expertise.

Dave Checketts . . . with a thank you for bringing me to New York and getting the Knicks under the salary cap.

Robert and Luisa Towne, Tom and Claire Calloway, and other dear friends.

There are the Showtime Warriors in business and in the professions whose conversations with me brought principles in this book to life. They include Michael Eisner, Michael Fuchs, Lod Cook, Teddy Forstmann, Bob Teufel, Jim Doyle, Jeff Morgan, Kenny Moore, David Stern, Dr. Rob Kerlan, Dr. Lew Richfield, and David Halberstam.

When a book project crosses the finish line, it's all too easy to forget how it all began, and I can't let that happen. Mort Janklow—without a doubt the premier agent in the book business—called HBO chairman Michael Fuchs. Mort knew that Michael was a friend and wanted Michael to ask me if I'd be interested in writing this book. So it all really began with a phone call bouncing off some satellite between two of the best-wired guys in the communications industry.

Putnam's CEO, Phyllis Grann, filled the project with fire and energy when she read the proposal and declared that Putnam wanted this book and had total faith in the concept. I have to particularly thank Putnam's publisher, Neil Nyren, for personally guiding the book's development. Neil is esteemed as one of the finest and most perceptive minds in the publishing industry. And I've learned why. Most of all, Neil did it all with the positive and gracious touch of a true champion. Finally, I must thank all the other colleagues at Team Putnam—marketing people, sales people, and all the other supporters and coordinators now ready to bring this book to the readers.

INTRODUCTION

Teamwork is the essence of life.

If there's one thing on which I'm an authority, it's how to blend the talents and strengths of individuals into a force that becomes greater than the sum of its parts. My driving belief is this: great teamwork is the only way to reach our ultimate moments, to create the breakthroughs that define our careers, to fulfill our lives with a sense of lasting significance.

This book is about a force that shapes us all—the desire to make our lives significant. It will encourage you to go for that ultimate prize. It will give you the right tools to get the job done. It will help you create an environment in which your talent can flourish.

I've had a long and well-rewarded career, connected with highly successful and accomplished people. Many of their stories are related in this book. Some revolve around championship-level basketball, some deal with other areas of human affairs, including high-stakes business dealings. All of them have a purpose: to help you blaze your own personal pathway to greatness, whatever you do in life.

All of us are team players, whether we know it or not. Our significance arrives through our vital connections to other people, through all the teams in our lives. Family life is a central team experience. Career teams may be a fledgling company or a department in a very large corporation, an industry leader or a struggling contender, a team of scientists or doctors or the faculty of a school. A neighborhood community action group is a team, and so is a congregation. You can be the one who lifts it, who sets the stage for its greatest accomplishments. That is what will make you great.

Every team is a stage setting, a place to act out the drama of our lives. When our teams excel, we win. Our best efforts, combined with those of our teammates, grow into something far greater and far more satisfying than anything we could have achieved on our own. Teams make us part of something that matters. They are the fountain from which all our rewards will ultimately flow.

HOWEVER—teamwork isn't simple. In fact, it can be a frustrating, elusive commodity. That's why there are so many bad teams out there, stuck in neutral or going downhill. Teamwork doesn't appear magically, just because someone mouths the words. It doesn't thrive just because of the presence of talent or ambition. It doesn't flourish simply because a team has tasted success.

The rhythms of teamwork have been the rhythms of my life. I was coached by legendary basketball masterminds. I played alongside Hall-of-Famers, as part of the winningest team ever, in any professional sport. I've coached some of the most outstanding players in the history of basketball. I was part of six championship teams as a head coach, assistant coach, and player. My present team has rebounded from years of adversity to become an acknowledged contender for 1990s greatness.

I've also enjoyed the good fortune to speak at a number of the world's most successful companies. That has put me together with people who lead multimillion- and multibillion-dollar businesses, who have shared experiences with me about what it takes to realize and sustain our dreams of success.

All of those contacts and experiences have proved to me, over and over again, that the complex inner rhythms of teamwork—flows of ambition, power, cooperation, and emotion—are the keys to making dreams come true. They have taught me, at the highest levels of competition, how to read the signs of potential change and growth within each team and each individual. They have illustrated that there are common challenges that every team, and every team player, must conquer on their road to significant achievement.

Under certain conditions, the dynamics within a team will evolve slowly, gradually, predictably. Under other circumstances, their changes come like quicksilver. The only certain fact, the one universal constant, is that they must change. When they do, you must be prepared. This book gives you tools, insights, and a plan of action that will allow you to make the most of any teamwork situation. It will help you become the one person who can lift a whole team.

Let me give just one example here. For me, no person epitomizes this team-lifting ability better than Earvin Johnson. During the 1990 Western Conference Finals, Earvin showed the remarkable depth of his team-leading instincts. It was game six, at the Forum, versus the Portland Trailblazers. With four seconds to go, the Lakers held a one-point lead. Portland was on the attack. A Laker defender suddenly knocked the ball loose and Earvin picked it up in the corner. Two Trailblazers rushed him, swiping at the ball and trying to rake it out of his hands. If they could get it back, they would have three seconds to make a game-winning shot.

In the hands of a talented team, a three-second possession has all the possibilities of an eternity. If they fouled Earvin, the officials would stop the clock. Even if he made the shots, Portland would still have three seconds to tie the game at the buzzer. And they had some very dangerous three-point shooters on the roster.

Any normal player would have wrapped his arms around the ball, denying the steal and taking the foul. Earvin didn't. He saw that four seconds were left on the arena clock, checked his own inner clock, and then lofted the ball toward the opposite end of the floor, where absolutely no one was waiting to receive it. He committed a deliberate turnover with the game on the line.

It seemed like a crazy move, and it stunned the crowd. But after the ball had described a two-story arc, bounded on the floor, and then thumped out of bounds, Portland was left with only about one second to shoot. Only then did a few see the sheer brilliance of what had just happened. An insurmountable ninety-four feet of floor gaped between Portland and the rim. Earvin's nowhere bouncing ball inscribed the Lakers' V for victory.

Kevin Loughrey, one of the great all-time shooting guards in the NBA, coined the saying: "You must shoot it up and sleep in the streets." It means that a shooting guard has to have enough confidence to take an open shot. If not, they might as well just quit. When the shots go in, they're heroes. When they don't, they could end up on cold pavement. They face the risks, they take the consequences. And, if they're good, they know how to rise above and beyond the risks consistently.

In your moments of challenge, you will need a vision of how to do just that, of how to go above and beyond. How to ride with the cycles of team change, making the most of every opportunity. How to draw out your natural leadership abilities until you become a Showtime Warrior—*The Winner Within* whose excellence is recognized, the one person who can make a difference for an entire team.

That's what this book is all about.

1

The Innocent Climb

"What's mine is yours, and what's yours is mine."
—*William Shakespeare*

"Ask not what your teammates can do for you.
Ask what you can do for your teammates."
—*Magic Johnson*

P eople are territorial animals. We all want to stake out something to call our own. We strike back when our turf is threatened. In business, and even in family life, we are caught up in constant and clever infighting: labor against management—marketing against accounting—child against parent.

Don't smother those territorial and competitive instincts. They're a vital part of your humanity. But harness them for the good of the team.

How does a team balance cooperation and competition? How does a team player or leader make fundamental forces such as the fighting instinct always work for him, instead of tearing the team apart?

The answer is to be found in *innocence*. Innocence? What? Let me tell you how.

On October 1st, 1991, one day before my very first training camp as coach of the New York Knicks opened, we acquired a tough, no-nonsense, highly aggressive, low-post player named Xavier McDaniel (he's since gone on to the Boston Celtics).

Xavier was an emotional, driven-to-dominate forward—tough and muscular—and his disposition was to dominate his opponent. Anyone who fits that description is also a very territorial individual. You can bank on it.

As it happened, we also had a like-minded first-year player already on the team, named Anthony Mason. Mace grew up on the tough streets of Queens, and from the instant the two laid eyes on one another, it was obvious that something was bound to happen. Each knew the other's reputation. Through the introductions and preliminaries that began training camp, the two men seemed to be circling one another.

Our first workout began with a no-contact rebounding drill. It was just supposed to be a way to teach technique. As chance would have it, McDaniel and Mason got paired up. Then, suddenly, eighteen minutes into my first practice as a New York Knick coach, all hell broke loose. We had a full-blown two-man riot on our hands. McDaniel was pounding both sides of Mason's head. Mason was answering with furious, lunging blows. It was one of those traveling fights: they collided under the basket, fought their way over to the sideline, then ricocheted out to the middle of the court. It finally ended as a draw.

And that was it. For the rest of the season, McDaniel and Mason were true teammates. Once they understood that they were both fierce com-

"Fortunate, indeed, is the man who takes exactly the right measure of himself . . ."
—Peter Mere Latham

petitors who wouldn't back down from intimida-
tion, the dispute ended. They respected each
other. They were ready to join their strengths for
the Knicks. They were ready to declare their innocence.

Let me explain what I mean. There's a tremendous difference between innocence and naiveté.
Some people never figure it out.

Being naive means failing to understand or ac-
knowledge the threats to your personal territory,
and it's pitiful. Most people get over being naive
very quickly, but then they go to the opposite extreme, to an exclusive focus on Number One, to
playing the angles and going for the end run. They
calculate before they give.

Being innocent means understanding territorial-
ity and knowing that each player has *his* space—
and then putting it aside for the good of the team.
The Xavier McDaniel–Anthony Mason story is
about suppressing territorial ego. It's a positive
choice. You make it for your own good, too—because trying too hard to be clever in defending
your turf makes for short-range thinking.

The greatest infighters, the league-leading self-
servers, always find a way to stab themselves with
their own daggers more deeply than they ever cut
an adversary.

Innocence is about trust in a team. It's an attitude: doing your most for the team will always
bring something good for you. It means believing
that everything you deserve will eventually come
your way. You won't have to grab for it. You won't
have to force it. It will simply catch up to you,
drawn along in the jetstream, the forward motion
of your hard work.

Not all teams behave fairly. Good people do

sometimes end up getting screwed, either by management or their own teammates. But by holding on to their beliefs, they'll eventually get aligned with the right management, the right teammates.

Innocence is a seed. The ground has to be ready, the season has to be favorable, time has to pass. But sooner or later that seed will flourish, and any team can begin what I call an innocent climb: a time of growth that unexpectedly changes the whole face of an organization. They say that the Chinese bamboo plant takes ten years for its root structure to establish itself properly, but once established, a bamboo plant can soar a hundred feet into the air in just a single year. Just like an innocent attitude, it will flourish sooner or later, given the right circumstances.

And, it's more than just innocence. *It's innocence with experience.* Only experienced innocence can combat the cynicism and pessimism so rampant these days.

It can happen on a brand-new team from day one, or it can rejuvenate one that has seen better days. Either way, it's a beautiful process. But it is an innocence with obligations. I can remember walking into the Portland Memorial Coliseum one day shortly after I was named the Lakers' coach.

"If the blind lead the blind, both shall fall into the ditch."
—*Matthew 15:14*

I headed up to the PR department to get some data, and suddenly found the entire team behind me. I waved them off and said, "Hey guys, you can go right to the locker room." But they stuck right with me. One of them said, "You're our leader. We follow." They were sending me a message about my new role, and it made an impression.

Experienced, responsible innocence has to have a conscious start. Let me give an example.

In the late 1970s, there was a General Motors manufacturing plant in Fremont, California, on the southeast side of San Francisco Bay—it was the struggling, next-to-last carmaking factory in a state that used to have five auto plants going full-time.

The GM Fremont plant was full of individuals who were great at protecting their own territories—at the expense of being winners.

The plant had been built back in 1962. People called it "the battleship." A gray, three-million-square-foot factory with a bunch of smokestacks, it simply looked like a big ship stranded on land. Before long, though, they called it the battleship for another reason: it was the scene of constant warfare between labor and management. GM kept spending millions to keep the facility up-to-date, but productivity kept going further and further down the tubes.

"We'd been trained to fight with management," Tony DeJesus, President of the United Auto Workers Local, said. "And management guys were trained to fight the Union. Both sides were good at it. We fought like hell."

In 1977 DeJesus led a wildcat strike, one of dozens of strikes, sick-outs, and shutdowns at Fremont.

Absenteeism was so far out of control, the line couldn't even start on time some mornings. Not enough people showed up.

In the late 1970s, the American auto industry was still healthy enough to absorb that kind of undisciplined, antiteamwork performance. Then along came 1980 and 1981, the biggest wake-up call in the industry's history. GM, Ford, and

Chrysler lost $5.5 billion to overseas competitors who made better cars at lower prices. Hundreds of thousands of UAW workers were laid off.

By 1982 the Fremont plant was on the verge of anarchy. Nearly two thirds of its workers were laid off. Labor-management battles were uglier than ever. Distrust ran so high that the labor contract was crammed with over four hundred pages of legal doublespeak. But it didn't serve as a basis for mutual understanding. Its details were the weapons cache that armed all their fights.

One day in March of 1982, GM put the battleship into mothballs. They closed the books on the worst disciplinary situation in the whole company. When they did, more than eight hundred union-filed grievances and sixty contested firings were part of the baggage they left behind.

"When elephants fight, it is the grass that suffers."
—*Kikuyu proverb*

That's what happens to teams in which everyone's first priority is to put a shell around his or her position, and to guard that domain against anyone breaking in. Teamwork requires that everyone's efforts flow in a single direction. Feelings of significance happen when a team's energy takes on a life of its own. When those feelings become the day-to-day reality of a team, nobody feels like leading strikes, sneaking off the job, or coming in late.

To the eyes of freeway passersby, Fremont must have looked like an industrial ghost town—empty, rusting, and rotting.

Or was it?

The people at the Fremont plant were presented a new chance, a fresh stab at innocence. Fortunately, they took it.

Here's how it came about.

While GM, Ford, and Chrysler struggled through

the early 1980s, Toyota rose quickly to become the world's third-ranked automaker. As a result, they came under pressure from the U.S. government to start making cars on American soil.

Meanwhile, GM decided it had to learn why Japanese car companies were so much more efficient and coordinated. And the United Auto Workers desperately needed to put its members into jobs. All three parties—successful Japanese managers, struggling American managers, and out-of-work American trade unionists—had been rattled enough to get down to basics and learn how to be a team.

The first step was the creation of a new entity: New United Motor Manufacturing, Inc., a joint venture that would begin building cars at the old Fremont plant. In February of 1983, GM agreed to provide the factory and to sell the cars. Toyota put up millions in cash and made a commitment to run the operation.

Next, the new venture—NUMMI, as it came to be called—had to come to terms with the UAW. Labor and management had to be restarted from scratch.

On September 21st, 1983, NUMMI and UAW signed a Letter of Intent. Unlike the epic-length contract of "battleship" days, this was a simple fifteen-page document. It talked about a spirit of cooperation. It promised wages and benefits equal to other U.S. auto workers. It said that if workers were laid off, executives would be laid off, too. NUMMI also promised to rehire many of the people who had worked at the plant before. They even trusted Tony DeJesus, the former strike leader, to help evaluate job candidates.

In return, the Union let go of something they had

"We must either find a way or make one."
—*Hannibal*

always thought essential. Previously, all the jobs at Fremont had been divided into a hundred different classifications. The idea had been to protect jobs, but the effect had been to slow the line to a crawl several times a day, while everyone waited for the "right" worker to come along and take care of a task anyone could have done.

Under the Letter of Intent, there were only four job classifications. Workers formed small teams. Everyone on the team spent equal time on each of the various tasks. By giving up the old system, they made the plant more efficient *and* they beat the awful old monotony. Absenteeism dropped to one tenth of what it had been.

By the fall of 1986, NUMMI workers had assembled more than two hundred thousand new cars and had been chosen by the Department of Labor for a case study in positive labor-management relations.

Newsweek called NUMMI "a model of industrial tranquillity."

Fortune deemed it "the most important labor relations experiment in the U.S. today."

Industry Week ranked the plant among America's twelve best manufacturing plants.

The Fremont plant had transformed itself.

Today, NUMMI pumps $300 million a year into the local economy. Between its own plant and all its suppliers, it generates close to five thousand jobs. To move that far from the old "battleship" days, a lot of people had to get out of their protective shells and *voluntarily combine their efforts, trusting in the outcome.*

Riles' Rule of Rebirth

In any dead-end situation, a team's members are ready for rebirth when:

- Survival instinct overrides territorial instinct.
- Being a part of success is more important than being personally indispensable.
- The team's energy and enthusiasm take on a life of their own.

If this big corporate rebirth sounds overwhelming, how about another example on a more personal scale? While the people in Fremont were trying to figure out how to survive, on the other side of the bay, a young San Francisco woman was facing a struggle of her own.

Cathy Sneed had been born into an African-American family of fourteen children. She'd been only eight when her mother died. At seventeen she dropped out of high school and hitchhiked to California. By age twenty-one she was on welfare, unmarried, struggling to raise two kids alone. Nevertheless, she got a college degree and landed a job counseling prisoners for the San Francisco Sheriff's Department.

Then, in 1982, a kidney disease struck. Two years of chemotherapy couldn't turn it around. Doctors gave up hope. Shortly before they checked her out of the hospital and sent her home to die, Sneed was visited by a co-worker from the Sheriff's Department. He brought a gift.

"Here," he said, tossing a copy of John Steinbeck's *The Grapes of Wrath* on her hospital bed. "You never read this because you were a punk in high school. Read it now."

She did. It made her think about the prisoners she had been working to help. Just like the people in the book, they were strong, independent people struggling to find a way out of hopelessness.

Steinbeck's characters found their redemption in working the land. Sneed latched on to the idea that the same thing could be true in real life. She guessed that in the simple act of helping something grow, inmates could start finding purpose.

Inside the fifty-year-old walls of the San Bruno Jail, she remembered, was a twelve-acre plot. Once it had been cultivated, but it had since grown full of weeds and become useless through neglect. To Sneed, it was a symbol for the discarded people inside the prison's walls. When her boss paid a call at the hospital, she made him commit to a promise: if she recovered, she would be allowed to bring the prison's acreage back to life.

"Believe that life is worth living and your belief will help create the fact."
—*William James*

Crime is the ultimate selfish act, she reasoned. People who became involved in crimes scarred themselves inside. It becomes harder and harder to change for the good—but maybe they could build their self-esteem, and that self-esteem could heal them.

Somehow, Sneed got over her sickness. She came back and worked side by side with a crew of four inmates to clear the land. They didn't have proper tools or experience in gardening. At one point they came across an enormous bramble bush blocking a patch of land. Sneed remarked, "If we could just move that bush, that's where I want to plant," and went off to borrow a carpenter's hammer, hoping to smash the big weed into smaller pieces. While she was gone, one of the inmates, a tattoo-covered drug offender, ripped the bush out with his bare hands. It was a primal act—getting down to basics and getting the job done. It proved how much positive energy was waiting to be tapped.

As could have been expected, in their first couple of weeks working on the garden, most prisoners would barely talk. They doggedly hung on to their jaded attitudes. But as soon as green young shoots began to break out of the brown dirt, they started smiling and asking questions, becoming more and more a part of a team, less and less like prisoners doing time. They found their best emotions and fed them into the work. In return, they got a profound psychological boost. They experienced an innocent climb.

Pulling the weeds was just like knocking out the obstacles they had met on the street—the drug dependencies, the pressure to join gangs, the easy-money paths of pimping, whoring, and dealing that always led to bigger and bigger doses of trouble. The young plants helped them understand their own ability to grow and to graft something new into their life.

An innocent climb, in its earliest stages, is just as fragile as any seedling. In too many cases, Cathy Sneed found, the process started in the prison garden reversed itself just as soon as an inmate was released to the streets. Negative currents reasserted their strength. Some of her people would show up in the obituaries column, others would simply turn up back in jail again. They would even say, "Cathy, I'm back, and I'm so glad." They were better off in prison than they were in their old neighborhoods.

The first ninety days after someone leaves jail are the most crucial. If an ex-prisoner can get something legitimate going right away, he or she has a good chance to break the cycle. But the transition is tough and the odds are long. Sneed wondered how the garden might make a more lasting impact.

Eventually, the way opened up. In the summer of 1990, the owner of a local bakery chain offered her the use of a half-acre of garbage-strewn, unused land behind his bakery, in a tough section of San Francisco. The Garden Project was born.

Sneed found a couple of houses to rent in the neighborhood, to create an in-between place where the positive change that had begun behind jail walls could be continued. She studied advanced gardening techniques so she could pass them on to the newly released prisoners. In turn, they tended their plants carefully, as if their own lives depended on it.

The businessman who donated the use of this land became The Garden Project's first client, buying fruits and herbs for his baked goods. Gourmet restaurants were impressed by the quality of the produce and started placing orders. Within two years, The Garden Project had a contract with the Department of Public Works to plant thousands of trees in San Francisco neighborhoods.

"Man's mind, stretched to a new idea, never goes back to its original dimensions."
—*Oliver Wendell Holmes*

And all because one woman decided that something had to be done. Hundreds of people have now progressed through The Garden Project that Cathy Sneed began. They raise over fifty thousand pounds of produce every year. More than ever before, the former prisoners are making a successful transition to independent jobs and new lives. They have found a hard-core connection between self-discipline and self-esteem and are abandoning a faded and cynical mindset. They give themselves to something, and they get rewarded with a sense of significance. In other words, they learn the foundation skill of *The Winner Within*—innocence.

Riles' Rule for Detecting Innocence
When a gifted team dedicates itself to unselfish trust and combines instinct with boldness and effort—it is ready to climb.

Nothing brought the importance of innocence home with more force than my own experiences with the stagnant Los Angeles Lakers of the late 1970s. They were seasoned pros, businesslike. They watched out—all too carefully—for their own territories, their own contracts, and their own individual financial security. On the court, they knew how to look good individually, but as a combined force they were only a competent, marginally exciting team.

The pattern of the Laker teams of the late 1970s was to finish in the middle of the playoff pack, drawing just enough fans to keep the bills paid. The owner, Jack Kent Cooke, was secretly negotiating to sell the franchise to Jerry Buss. The coach, Jerry West, was so frustrated trying to wake up the enormous potential within the team that he announced he wouldn't be back. Eventually Jerry was to become the general manager. At the time, I was working for the Laker organization as a television analyst, traveling secretary, and producer of personality profiles for halftime features.

About the only cause for excitement in the spring of 1979 was the fact that the Lakers would pick first in the draft. Out of Lansing, Michigan, came the guy they wanted and needed: an unconventionally tall point guard at 6'9", only nineteen years old, and named Earvin Johnson. He was clearly a phenomenal player, and his skills were so finely honed that his abilities almost seemed magical. While he became "Magic" to the fans, he has always remained Earvin to his close friends and "Buck" to his teammates. Whatever the name, there was no doubt that this young man brought something with him not visible on the surface.

"Why do you want to come to this team?" a reporter asked him at his first Los Angeles press conference. "You don't even know who your coach will be."

"I enjoy the game so much," he answered, "I don't care who the coach is or what he asks of me." And then he added: "If my teammates will let me, I'd like to be a leader."

"Power is not revealed by striking hard or often, but by striking true."
—*Honoré de Balzac*

What was this? A player who didn't think of himself first? But he *was* thinking of himself. Magic Johnson believed that if he helped everyone around him get what they wanted out of the game, then winning would always follow.

And so would his own rewards, in their own time and of their own accord.

The Lakers already had some great veteran talent. Kareem Abdul-Jabbar was on his way to becoming the greatest scorer in NBA history. Point Guard Norm Nixon was among the league leaders in steals and assists. Jamaal Wilkes averaged close to twenty points a game, and Michael Cooper was about to break onto the scene and become the greatest sixth man in the game.

But, as Irving Berlin said about another competitive field, "Talent is only a starting point in this business." Would the addition of one green nineteen-year-old be enough—no matter what his attitude?

Every player has a style—a certain collection of choices and tendencies that flows through his entire game. An exceptional player usually demands that the team's personnel and game plan revolve around his style, so his performance can flourish and he can be recognized as a great star. Whenever a clash erupts within a team, it's usually over who gets to put his individual stamp on the team's identity, who will occupy the center ring of the big circus.

Riles' Rule on Style

The biggest battle on a pro court is the one between style and efficiency. A particular shot or way of moving the ball can be a player's personal signature, but efficiency of performance is what wins the game for the team. Style can juice the player and stir the crowd, but it must never overwhelm the fundamental goal of playing the game and winning.

Earvin had both style and efficiency and knew when to let one dominate over the other. He quickly established himself as a dominant player, but he did it in a unique way. He was an avid student of all the styles of basketball. Instead of crushing his teammates under his own greatness, he studied *their* styles and figured out how he, as the man controlling the movement of the ball, could help them get the most out of the abilities they had. He dealt to their strengths.

His first pro road game provided a glimpse of the change he was to bring to the team's outlook. The San Diego Clippers were a second-division team, but they got into a position to steal our season opener. Kareem—as he had done so many times in his career—pulled the game out at the buzzer, arching in one of his deadly skyhooks from twenty feet. Then, completely expressionless, he turned and headed for the shower. It was the way Kareem enjoyed winning. Before he could reach the far end of the court, however, Magic came bounding over. He hurled himself into the center's arms, hugged him with all his exuberant might, and poured praise on his captain.

Kareem couldn't believe what was going on. This was just the first night of an eighty-two-game, nine-month stretch. Didn't this rookie have any sense of cool?

No, he didn't. He had fire. Which was something this all-too-professional team had been needing. He shared it with every man on the floor, through so many nights of double-figure scoring, rebounding and assists that reporters started calling him "Mr. Triple-Double." Eventually, he made those seasoned pros catch fire along with him. All year long, he showed a rare ability, something on which every commentator since has remarked over and over: he made all his teammates better.

We rode this innocent shuttle to a great season, and finished with sixty wins, just one win shy of the best record in the NBA. Then we began to tear through the playoffs, eventually ending up against Philadelphia in the finals.

The MVP of the series looked to be Abdul-Jabbar. Kareem, whom people claimed had lost his passion for basketball, played the most impressive series of his entire life, and behind him we won three of the first five games—before disaster struck.

Late in the third quarter of that fifth game, Kareem severely sprained his ankle and had to be

"Great men are meteors designed to burn so that earth may be lighted."
—*Napoleon*

taken off the court. Knowing that we needed his production, the trainer retaped the ankle, and Kareem went back in for the fourth quarter. He scored forty points, fourteen of them in the fourth quarter.

Page one of the next day's *L.A. Times* carried a banner headline: KAREEM WON'T PLAY FRIDAY.

When the team flew to Philly for game six, Kareem rested at home, propping his injured ankle on a pillow, hoping it would heal quickly. In the Big Fella's absence, everyone assumed, the 76ers would dominate and send the series back to the Forum for a winner-take-all showdown. There was only one question left: could Kareem get healthy in time for Game Seven?

At practice, one of our starters told me, "There's no way we can win in Philadelphia. I want to stay behind and rest up for the seventh game."

On any team trip, Kareem always used to claim seat 1-A in the plane's first-class compartment. It was one of the team's unspoken rules. This time, though, Magic—a star, but nonetheless just a rookie—took the captain's seat. It was audacious, but it was also wonderfully innocent:

"We're missing Kareem? Okay, fellas—I'll be Kareem today."

Then, just as he had on the airplane and with Coach Westhead's blessing, Magic took the captain's place at the opening tipoff by jumping center. Throughout the game, he alternated between guard, center, and forward. He scored from each position, and he inspired the others to play in the same way—as if we had nothing to lose. We were loose-jointed, having a great time. Guys who seldom got off the bench put in some of the best minutes of their lives. Behind Magic's forty-two

"I just want to let you know that if nobody wants this job, I'm happy to take it."
—*Pat Riley, volunteering for the position of Lakers' head coach at a press conference*

points, game six became a 123–107 blowout, our widest victory margin in the entire series. The Lakers became world champions, on the shoulders of a guy who still hadn't seen his twenty-first birthday.

The next day, sports page headlines blared IT WAS MAGIC.

It wasn't really magic. It was just Earvin achieving his dream, showing that one person can make a difference.

One afternoon in the summer of 1980, I told Earvin that in more than twenty years of playing and coaching basketball, I'd never seen such a complete package—great skills combined with great attitude. I asked him point-blank: "Why are you the way you are? Why do you give everything away?"

And Earvin told me about something that had happened when he was a little boy, playing Youth League basketball in East Lansing, Michigan.

Early in the season, his coach had taken him aside and said "You're the biggest. You're our best player. You should shoot the ball all the time."

He'd done as he was told. Because he was so gifted, he scored most of the points every game. His team won, time after time. But when he looked around at the moment of victory, hoping someone would return that big smile of his, his teammates looked miserable. They felt like nobodies. The coach's game plan was producing wins, but it was bashing the team's feelings of success and significance.

Earvin didn't want it to be that way. It drove a wedge between him and his friends. So he decided to change his style. Instead of scoring all the points, he would draw the defenders, then pass to

"The best way to cheer yourself up is to cheer everybody else up."
—*Mark Twain*

whoever was open. Through this unselfishness he would enhance the skills of others. He would help them experience the same kind of kinetic, contagious joy from playing that he always felt. Then they'd be motivated to be their best. The team could experience both winning and success at the same time.

That was when the Lakers' surge to glory *really* began—when Magic Johnson was just a kid. It worked then. It was still working at age twenty. The Lakers' 1980 championship was not only a great triumph, it was the team's first step toward becoming a dynasty. It had begun its innocent climb—and it had all started with one person.

What about you—your life, your business, your neighborhood? Are you the Magic Johnson or Cathy Sneed who can make the difference? Do you have the courage to put aside ego and turf wars for the common good, as they did at New United Motors?

They believed in the power of innocence. Can you?

Time-Out

At the end of each chapter, we'll take a break and sum up where *The Winner Within* has taken us up to now. So far, we've learned that an Innocent Climb begins when a team comes together unselfishly, its members often not having had the past experience of great success, and unexpectedly achieves dramatic things. A team in an Innocent Climb can feel the power surging, so internal rivalries, turf wars, and selfish behavior patterns are set aside.

2

The Disease
of Me

"Self-interest is the enemy of all true affection."
—*Tacitus*

"It requires a strong constitution to withstand
repeated attacks of prosperity."
—*J. L. Basford*

A moment in the movie *Wall Street* crystallized for me the biggest reason why teams break down. The scene was a large corporate meeting, being held in some vast room, with hundreds of business men and women in attendance. Stodgy, anonymous company managers argued with the shareholders for patience, but profits were down. In a sensible world, these forces should have been working with each other. Instead, each special-interest group wanted results that would benefit itself. A corporate raider grabbed a hand-held microphone and took over the meeting. Everything about his clothing and his manner told you that he was successful, self-assured, in command. His message boiled down to three seductive words: "Greed is good."

The movie was fictional, but the phrase came

"Anybody who gets away with something will come back to get away with a little bit more."
—*Harold Schoenberg*

directly from a real-life speech that was delivered to a group of college students by someone who, for a short time, was considered one of America's most astute businessmen. He went on to become one of the most famous prisoners of the Federal judicial system. So did a number of other greed-driven financiers for their dealings in the paired phenomena of insider trading and junk-bond-financed corporate buyouts.

That phrase, "Greed is good," represented a way of thinking that became rampant. People were deemed fools unless they grabbed for everything they could get. Little signposts everywhere in the popular culture announced it—slogans declaring how "You only go around once in life," slogans asking, "Who says you can't have it all?" For much of the 1980s, greed defined the tone of the times. We're just beginning to understand fully how much this greed orgy cost us all as a nation, as a team.

Greed seduced the Lakers, too, right at the start of the 1980s. It led our team into subconscious sabotage. Their Innocent Climb was a once-in-a-lifetime phenomenon. But the aftermath of early victory placed everything in peril.

Unless you learn to manage the aftereffects of winning, the forces that led your team to the top will turn around and destroy you. The Lakers were a team that had won a championship, but they weren't a championship team, and they weren't to become one until they overcame the great barriers to truly winning from within. The first of those was: The Disease of Me.

While the Lakers of 1980 were World Champions all right, a little bit of adversity and a whole lot of greed-is-good thinking drew us into one of the quickest falls in the history of the NBA. We were making plans to repeat as champions, but—without realizing it—we were tearing our own team apart at the same time. The inside story of what went on within the 1980–1981 Lakers is an incredible parallel to what happened in American society during the 1980s, especially in the world of finance. However, the parallel timing was more coincidence than not. The Disease of Me is poised to strike any winning team in any year and at any moment. The good news: while it's ever present, it *can* be overcome . . . and most of all *it can be anticipated.*

When the Disease of Me afflicts the strongest members of a team, or even its coaches, they develop an overpowering belief in their own importance. Their actions virtually shout the claim, "I'm the one." They try to prove that they really are as important as the fawning press and idolizing fans think. It doesn't take long for such antics to be transparent in a professional team sport. But, in business more than in basketball, it's possible to conceal the weakness or the problems of the organization hooked to a "star."

"Selfishness is the only real atheism; aspiration, unselfishness the only real religion."
—*Israel Zangwill*

Because personal performers such as the publisher Robert Maxwell and petroleum baron Armand Hammer were masters at courting the business press, the financial community, and other powerful outsiders, their businesses seemed to many much stronger than they actually were. When they passed away, the world was in for a rude awakening. It is much harder to truly act alone and succeed today in the way that entrepreneurs such as Thomas Edison or Henry Ford did in times past. Even the apparently maverick commodity trader of today is working with an intricate network of information sources and analytic support.

When the Disease of Me infects the weakest members of a team, the people who create about 20 percent of the team's effectiveness feel shut out from the spotlight. They come to believe that they're really deserving of 80 percent of the rewards, and develop a tunnel-visioned fixation on upping their share of the material take.

I call this *Riles' Rule of the Reverse 20/80.* This rule is rooted in one of the basics of modern marketing, and it's true for almost any company in any industry: eighty percent of the sales come from 20 percent of the products offered . . . or 20 percent of a firm's sales force. The 20 percent are the blockbusters, while the 80 percent merely fill out the line or the work force and give customers a choice . . . or the perception of one. Today, companies are feeling a lot of pressure to control inventory costs and to keep their assortments lean, but the 80–20 rule still holds for the most part.

Riles' Rules of the Reverse 20/80

When a successful organization becomes infected with the Disease of Me, people who create 20 percent of the results will begin believing they deserve 80 percent of the rewards.

The greater a single teammate's success, the stronger the resentment can be from the weakest 20 percent. The performance Earvin Johnson gave in the final game of the 1980 playoffs was possibly the greatest single game any pro basketball player ever had. Naturally, the public and the media exulted over what this young rookie had done. Rewards zoomed to him like iron filings to a magnet. He became the toast of L.A. His face was everywhere—in magazines and newspapers, on billboards and on television. The more Magic was elevated or lionized, the smaller some World Champion Lakers felt in comparison. During the off-season, it was hard to see this coming. For some of us, the summer seemed a laid-back time to bask in the glory of our championship. But hidden agendas were coming to the forefront, signalizing the outbreak of the Disease of Me.

As we reassembled, you could have read the first symptom of the fledgling Disease as the very glow of health and well-being. The day training camp opened, everyone was surprised to see one core player arrive in the best shape of his career. A couple of years earlier, when he'd come to us from another team, he'd had a roll of fat around his waist. Now his physique looked hand-carved. But his motivation for secretly working out all summer wasn't simply driven by how much more he could give the team. It was for personal gain. He wanted to show he could challenge the greatest offensive weapon in the history of the NBA, Kareem Abdul-Jabbar. Sometimes a rising challenge within a team creates healthy change. It spurs everyone to do their best and to prove their worth. Was this the drive for excellence or a selfishness of spirit? In this case it was the latter—a lightning rod for the resentment gathering between teammates.

> "The force of selfishness is as inevitable and as calculable as the force of gravitation."
> —Hailliard

As he later said in his book, *Giant Steps*, Kareem believed that he, not Earvin, should have been voted MVP of the 1980 finals. A handful of players resented Kareem's "otherness" and they formed a clique against him and his idiosyncrasies.

As soon as drills began, Kareem figured out what was in the wind, and he intimidated the hell out of everybody who physically challenged him.

The ambitious core player's bid for leadership was very short-lived, but it put a dynamic into motion. Indeed, Kareem's obvious victory scarred Kareem himself. Despite any appearances to the contrary, Kareem wants to be liked and respected, just like anyone else. But the challenge to his leadership hurt him, and made an already aloof individual even more distant from his teammates. The clique had to draw a bead on another target for their frustrations.

In a second corner, all by himself, sat another core player. Although he wasn't part of the clique, he wasn't aligned with anyone else, either. He had given the best performance of his own All-Star career in the championship-winning game at Philadelphia, yet had been almost ignored in the excitement surrounding Magic.

Between the cliques, the hurt feelings, and the petty jealousies, the Lakers suddenly had a leadership vacuum at the top of the team, and a negative force field in the ranks. Here was a carbon copy of the interpersonal situation that you'll find in the day-to-day life of most offices or factories, or even some families. It's the grist of melodramas and soap operas, and it's what keeps *The Winner Within* corked up like a genie in a bottle. But in our case there was a difference.

This script was being played out under the klieg lights of sudden, highly visible success—and sudden success intensifies this pressure tenfold. Those of the 20 percent effective set out after the 80 percent rewards with a vengeance. Greed cruised to the surface—attacking the disciplines, the collaboration, and the flow that enabled us to succeed in the first place.

Public pressure can rile the Disease of Me like an icy draft can make pneumonia out of a common cold. The team began its 1980–1981 season considered likely to win the first back-to-back NBA championships since 1969. The press had yet to sense the brewing turmoil: a sportswriter who rode the team bus during the early weeks of the season described a loose, happy atmosphere among our players. We hadn't lost two consecutive games in over a year. Earvin was scoring more than ever before, creating more steals and assists than anyone else in the NBA, while pulling down more rebounds than any other guard. On the surface, things glistened. On buses, you could hear the players singing "Love X Love" by George Benson.

Finally, the first public crisis unfolded for Coach Westhead. Earvin was then, as he was throughout his career, an all-out player. He took a lot of bangs and bruises. About two weeks into the season, a seven-foot center fell across the back of his left knee. A couple of days later, an opposing forward collided with that same knee. Less than a week later, early in the second quarter of a game, something inside his knee popped and he fell down in a heap. His medial semilunar cartilage was torn. Surgery was needed immediately, followed by a three-month recuperation. Jerry Buss, the team owner, went beyond the doctor's orders and ordered Magic out for a full 100 days. Even then, the public still saw a positive team attitude: "This will be another test for us," One of the Lakers told the *L.A. Times*. "It'll show what we are really made of."

He was speaking more truth than he could possi-

"Success has ruined many a man."
—*Ben Franklin*

bly realize. The first part of the test—stepping up and playing our best, despite having one less superstar to pull us through—was actually the easiest. The crucial part came later, and it was a test of more than our basketball ability. It was a test of our spirit of togetherness and our character. Afflicted by the Disease of Me, it was a test we were destined to fail.

We lost five games in a row after Earvin's injury. Gradually, though, the remaining players pulled together, adjusted, and won twenty-eight of their next forty. That translates to winning 70 percent of the time, which is outstanding performance. Michael Cooper started alongside Nixon, and they both had several big nights. Inspired by showing what they could do without the guy who had, overnight, become the focus of fans, media, and management, the Lakers held on to a strong second place in the Pacific Division.

This great level of accomplishment actually worsened the Disease of Me because the players grew convinced that no one knew how well they were really doing. So intense was Earvin's stardom that his absence seemed more newsworthy than their wins. As his return grew closer, during the time-outs near the end of every home game the public address announcer would always say, "And don't forget to mark your calendars—Friday, February 27th. Magic Johnson returns to the lineup of your World Champion Los Angeles Lakers!" The players, hearing this, would look up from their huddle and shake their heads, as if to say "F——— that. We're winning *now!*"

The Laker organization was so eager to market the excitement of Earvin's return that they forgot about motivating the guys who were getting the job done on the court. Their *own* specialness was being drained away, and maintaining that special-ness is something for which leadership is always accountable. Earvin himself praised the results the team was achieving, but his voice was drowned out by the fuss over his absence and by the power of the marketing mechanism.

Riles' Rule: Getting the Best of the Bench

The team on the court is the team of the moment. When the first string snaps, motivate the players you have, rather than moaning about the players you don't have. You'll never rouse *The Winner Within* by making people feel they're only a fill-in for side-lined greatness.

The dam finally burst. One of our starters got fed up with the hoopla and told a reporter, "He's just one guy. He's special—he has great instincts and ability—but we're a team!" Still, the promotional frenzy went forward relentlessly, coming to a head on the night of February 27th. As they clicked through the turnstiles, each of the 17,505 ticket holders was handed his or her own "The Magic Is Back" button. There was a drawing set for half time: grand prize—a Magic Johnson jogging suit. At least fifty press photographers crowded the floor while the players were introduced. Normally, only the starters' names are called. Even though Earvin was going to be on the bench when the game began, he was included in the introductions. At the mere mention of his name, the Forum rocked with a standing ovation. Dozens of camera-men took positions at his feet and fired away. The whole thing flared to outsize proportions: the Magic Man was back. He would lead us to the Promised Land.

Meanwhile, the guys who had carried the team for three months were seething with resentment.

We were up against the New Jersey Nets, who sat near the basement of the entire league. We opened raggedly, quickly falling behind by five points. Then Coach Westhead signaled Earvin out on the floor and the arena erupted. As soon as he got in, though, he threw a pass straight to a defender, then another one out of bounds. He missed his first two shots. Between Earvin's rustiness and the halfhearted play of some of his teammates, we barely hung on for a four-point win.

After the game, reporters circled around Earvin, ignoring the rest of the team, questioning him for half an hour. Finally he said, "Now I think all of you can leave me alone." But they wouldn't. An hour later, all the other players had gone home, and half a dozen reporters were still in a semicircle around the star of the evening. Earvin tried to divert their praise and give credit to his teammates, but that wasn't the story they were after.

Over the last seventeen games of the season, the Lakers were a divided team, with a splinter group of guys who were just trying to deflect the reality of the conflict—clocking in and out of the job without getting involved. I had already seen lots of aggravated situations in my NBA career—including a championship-winning team that fought over money at its own victory party.

"By union the smallest states thrive. By discord the greatest are destroyed."
—Sallust

What had started with the collapse of team commitment was becoming team sabotage. Most team sabotage begins on a subconscious level. It starts with emotional decisions—flare-ups that twist actions away from the good of the team. Unless stopped, those wrong-minded actions take on a life of their own. Eventually the team is divided against itself—ready to shatter under any pressure, any adversity.

The loose, cheerful Lakers team that reporters had written about in November had a totally different look about them in March, when our season ended with two straight losses. Before, the closeness was openly visible—in the constant free exchanges of high fives, in the smiles on everyone's faces after a win. By the playoffs, we were just a collection of paid professionals. We did what was required and then we split.

Game one of the three-game opening round was scheduled for April Fool's Day against the Houston Rockets. They weren't an outstanding team, even with the great Moses Malone at center. They had won less than 50 percent of their regular-season games. Our talent level was far more impressive. We held home-court advantage. Both teams started tall lineups, hoping to counteract each other's strengths, but Malone was unstoppable. He went berserk with thirty-eight points and twenty-three rebounds. We got whipped on our home court, 111–107. C-R-A-C-K!!! One loss and THE LOOK!

This was serious business. We had to win the next two to stay alive. Forget about the pride at stake or our fading opportunity to win back-to-back championships, the Laker organization stood to lose millions of dollars in projected playoff ticket sales. Meanwhile, our dissension was no longer a secret. Quotes, attributed to "sources close to the team," appeared in newspaper stories on the morning of game two. Paul Westhead changed the lineup. Chones out. Cooper in. And we tightened down to a smaller core.

We jumped to an early 18–5 lead, then slowly extended it to twenty points before we let up and allowed the Rockets to claw their way back. They came within three points in the last three minutes, but we kept our grip and emerged with a win.

Game three would be at the Forum, winner-take-all.

The next morning, alongside the writeup of our win was another story. This was the lead paragraph: "The joy is missing from the Lakers this time around. And no one feels that vacuum more keenly than the one who made the Lakers joyful in the first place—Magic Johnson. It has recently occurred to Johnson that some of his teammates have come to resent him." The seeds were planted.

Members of the anti-Johnson clique were asked for quotes. They denied the ill feelings, but their words rang hollow. The story ended on an ominously accurate note—"The Lakers have seen the enemy, and they have the uneasy feeling that it is them."

"The moment we break faith with one another, the sea engulfs us and the light goes out."
—*James Baldwin*

Game three was scheduled at 12:30 in the afternoon on Sunday, April 5th. I remember walking out of my office an hour before the tipoff, pausing a moment in the press lounge to grab the last three french fries from the buffet table, then walking downstairs to the team's dressing room. Once I got there, I opened the door on one of the most painful and inappropriate things I've ever seen. A full-blown argument was going on about what had been reported in the papers.

While younger players hurled accusations at each other, two of our starters, in opposite corners of the room, laced on their basketball shoes and kept their heads down. They were disgusted with the scene and wanted no part of it. As veterans, they couldn't believe something so wrong could be happening to a team just minutes before an all-important game.

True team veterans know that there can only be one state of mind as you approach any profound test: total concentration, a spirit of togetherness, and strength. The young players were facing more than they could stand, and instinct led them to try putting things right by bringing the conflict into the open. (Countless companies tried this free-form kind of openness in the seventies and eighties in poorly managed gripe sessions and saw it fail as tough problems and complaints were raised that management couldn't answer.)

Our game focus was gone. It didn't matter that we were the defending champs, coming in with one of the top records in the NBA, or that the Rockets had the lowliest record of any team in the playoffs. In a make-or-break situation, with our pursuit of back-to-back championships on the line, all our guys could give was an uninspired effort. A few seconds before the final buzzer, two Lakers failed to communicate on a simple defensive switch. Mike Dunleavy, a Houston guard with a great shooting touch, got left wide open, and sank a jump shot that put the Rockets one point ahead.

We had one last chance to win it. Coach West-head brought the team into a final huddle. He diagrammed a play for Earvin to get the ball to Kareem in the low post for a hook shot. When we broke huddle, there was a distant look in Earvin's eyes. His mind was turning in a whole different direction.

It was no secret that Earvin still felt himself to be

the target of much hostility. He brought the ball across half court and dribbled four times, surveying the defense. It seemed as though a thought crossed his mind: "Maybe if I take the initiative and I score, the guys will appreciate me again." He went spinning through the center of the lane, bumping against a Houston player, hoping to draw a foul as he finger-rolled the final shot of our season. No whistles blew. The ball never touched rim or backboard. It dropped right into the hands of Moses Malone.

We lost. It wasn't Earvin's fault. It was just the Disease of Me coming to its inevitable result: the Defeat of Us.

In time, after conquering their own early-1980s excesses, the Lakers would also achieve phenomenal, even astronomic accomplishments. But first they had to reap the bitter embarrassment that their selfishness had created. Only twice before in NBA history had a defending champ gone down in the first playoff round: it happened to the 1957 Philadelphia Warriors and the 1949 Baltimore Bullets. Because of greed, pettiness, and resentment, we executed one of the fastest falls from grace in NBA history.

There was even more adversity in store for the Lakers. But we got beyond it, just as any team can, and learning to recognize the symptoms of the disease affecting us was a major reason why.

Seven Danger Signals of the Disease of Me

- Inexperience in dealing with sudden success.
- Chronic feelings of underappreciation.
- Paranoia over being cheated out of one's rightful share.

- Resentment against the competence of partners.
- Personal effort mustered solely to outshine a teammate.
- A leadership vacuum resulting from the formation of cliques and rivalries.
- Feelings of frustration even when the team performs successfully.

What about the teams in your life? Are they due for a checkup? Do you still have time to prevent The Disease of Me?

The most difficult thing for individuals to do when they're part of the team is to sacrifice. It's so easy to become selfish in a team environment. To play for me. It's very vulnerable to drop your guard and say, "This is who I am and I'm gonna open up and give of myself to you." But that's exactly what you've got to do. Willing sacrifice is the great paradox. You must give up something in the immediate present—comfort, ease, recognition, quick rewards—to attract something even better in the future: a full heart and sense that you did something which counted.

Without that sacrifice, you'll never know your team's potential, or your own.

Time-Out

Let's recap. The Innocent Climb—success through unselfishness—has been shattered by the Disease of Me. The team is awash in petty rivalries. Greed and resentment eat away at the team's togetherness and undermine its ability to collaborate. Factions divide the loyalties within the team. Personal performance slides. No matter how fast an Innocent Climb uplifted a team, the Disease of Me cuts it down even quicker.

3

The Core Covenant

"To be trusted is a greater compliment
than to be loved."
—*George MacDonald*

"We must all hang together,
else we shall all hang separately."
—*Benjamin Franklin*
on signing The Declaration of Independence

Right after the 1992 NBA season ended, my wife Chris and I, along with five couples and six others, were invited by some dear friends to paddle down the Colorado River in a twelve-foot inflatable raft loaded with six days' worth of camping provisions. Instead of the roar of Madison Square Garden, our ears reverberated with the rapids gushing through the Grand Canyon. As we hit the first few yards of a white water run, the raft began bucking and pitching. Wilder rapids were looming up ahead. Suddenly, instead of paddling, just keeping the raft from turning sideways and tumbling over became the number-one priority. The closer we got to the big rocks, the more it became a full-time job.

Outside of the professional guides who did this for a living, the rest of us didn't have to be there.

To tell the truth, we in the crew were kind of a privileged group. Between our raft and eight other rafts on the same expedition, there were several very successful people from high-profile occupations—top film and music executives, famous actors, people who owned companies worth millions, and other professional entrepreneurs—the kind of people who usually had staff to take care of life's basic chores. Some of this group—us included—probably hadn't packed our own suitcase, washed our own dishes, or turned on our own bathwater in years. But the voyage gave us a real sense of confronting nature; and, by the end of the second day, we had started calling ourselves by the moniker The Scorpions.

"Mutual aid is as much a law of animal life as mutual struggle."
—*Prince Kropotkin*

The river was a great equalizer. We were all in this together, in an intensely democratic setting. Each of us carried nothing beyond bare necessities and each needed to shoulder one hundred percent of our own weight and responsibility.

As we rushed toward a midriver boulder, my side of the raft rose up and draped itself around the rock's edge. The raft passed the boulder, my side slapping the river as it sprang back. I suddenly thought about one of the "Rules of the River," the short lessons our guides had taught us when we shoved off from the peaceful riverbank two days earlier. "If you fall overboard," they said, "YOU MUST BE AN ACTIVE PARTICIPANT IN YOUR OWN RESCUE."

There were only a few Rules of the River, but everyone had to respect them completely. They could be the difference between drowning and staying alive. That's why this collection of people who were used to being pampered and indulged suddenly became a society of equals. Everyone put their back into their paddle stroke. Everyone did their fair share of hauling and cleaning at every night's encampment.

The Rules of the River formed a simple covenant. Following them made us a together team. Whenever we reached placid water, we could afford to tilt our heads back and stare at the bands of centuries-old color in the high rock walls. Sometimes we floated for miles listening to Placido Domingo tapes jacked up full-tilt. We felt almost as much awe and satisfaction in our own accomplishment and our teamwork, in the success of our covenant, as we did in marveling over the Grand Canyon itself.

A Covenant is an agreement that binds people together. Sometimes a Covenant is written out in great detail. Sometimes it is unspoken, completely expressed through action or trust. Every team develops Covenants over time, through simply being together. But some Covenants are better than others, and a number of Covenants are actually destructive. Flawed Covenants are often built on negativity and insidious behavior. That's why there are so many bad teams out there. Any team afflicted with the Disease of Me functions with a tacit Covenant of self-destruction.

The Constructive Covenant

   . . . binds people together,

   . . . creates an equal footing,

   . . . helps people shoulder their own responsibilities,

   . . . prescribes terms for the help and support of others,

   . . . and creates a foundation for teamwork.

The most profound Core Covenant I know of, the Declaration of Independence, reverberates with these words: "We hold these truths to be self-evident: That all men are created equal; that they are endowed by their creator with certain inalienable rights."

Every team that wants to move toward significance and greatness has to decide what truths it will hold to be self-evident and to get those values circulating throughout the organization.

Riles' Rule of the Heart

Every team must decide, very consciously, to uphold Covenant terms that represent the best of values—voluntary cooperation, love, hard work, and total concentration on the good of the team. The greatness flowing through the heart of the team must be pumped out to all the extremities.

The Core Covenant must spring from the natural leaders and spread throughout the team. The top producers, being the team's natural leaders, the ones that rookies and second-stringers inherently want to follow, have to be the source of that Covenant. They have to monitor the rest and to apply positive peer pressure.

People sometimes ask me, "What would you rather have, a winning team or a together team?"

When you understand team dynamics, it's obvious: A team must first be *together*—like a sound, strong family. People on all levels of the team, from parent to child, from foreman to assembler, from superstar to role player, have to endorse—and uphold—a Core Covenant.

Strong Covenants are generally forged in crisis,

and the closing months of 1981 put the Lakers through a make-or-break test. At several points they faced the possibility of dissolving and completely cashing in their dreams of being a significant team. Now the Lakers are known as the Team of the Decade in the eighties. But for a few months we were very close to being instant has-beens.

The 1980–1981 Lakers had operated with a destructive Covenant, an unspoken agreement which you can find on lots of teams—that it was okay to put the team second if you felt wronged or jealous. One consequence of our 1981 playoff disgrace was that a few unhappy players got shipped out. To fill the gap created at power forward, we went after Mitch Kupchak, a strapping, hardworking player with good scoring and rebounding numbers, who brought a great attitude as well. But Kupchak's acquisition stirred controversy, too. We needed what Kupchak provided, but his price was high. Free agents were just beginning to draw big contracts then, and Mitch's deal upset players on the Lakers and all around the league—"If that's what *he's* worth, what about *me?*"

> "Jealousy, the jaundice of the soul."
> —*John Dryden*

We got a bigger dose of the same kind of negative attitude when, in midsummer, team owner Jerry Buss signed Earvin Johnson to a twenty-five-year, $25-million contract. At that point in history, it was the richest deal any athlete had ever signed. For Buss it was nothing but a shrewd move. Earvin's original contract was due to expire soon. Anyone with an eye for talent realized that his price would only go higher.

Several of our players arrived at training camp definitely downbeat. Some were still discouraged by our playoff embarrassment. Some were sore about the gap between their paychecks and those of Earvin, who now seemed to be the Lakers' favorite son, and Mitch. One veteran, who still had many more good playing years left in him, was so upset that we had to talk him out of quitting.

The disappointment and dissension began to be focused—undeservedly so—on the head coach, Paul Westhead. The players were in pain. They wanted that pain salved, and they talked themselves into believing he was its source. He wasn't. Our team's problems all came from inside.

A team that hasn't committed itself to a positive Covenant is always fragile at best. On the surface, everything may look fine—as long as there's smooth sailing. But you're always just one ego, one disagreement, one rough patch away from disintegration. We were in that fragile state. Trust had gone into eclipse. The players were afraid of being caught weak and alone, and worried about which faction they should join.

"A house divided against itself cannot stand."
—*Abraham Lincoln*

Little groups convened in hotel rooms to carp about the people in management or those in the other cliques. Stories hit the paper, saying "key Laker players" were frustrated with how they were being told to play. Later on, the media unjustly portrayed Earvin Johnson as a ringleader of the dissent. He was actually one of the least outspoken.

This is what happens whenever people on a team decide not to trust: everyone will gear down their effort until they're doing just enough to get by. They want, subconsciously, to enroll everyone else in their cycle of disappointment. They'll be too smart to mess up enough to be singled out, but their subtle withholding of effort may eventually be enough to bring about a systemwide failure.

You could see those rips and tears in our team as

the season arrived. Our opening game was against Houston, the same team that had beaten us in the first round. We were down three as the final seconds ticked off. Earvin sent up a desperation three-pointer that sent us into overtime and raised our hopes, but eventually we gave the game away. Discouragement built over the next two weeks, as we won two games and lost three. San Antonio blew us out of our sixth game, 128–102.

As the players filed on board the team bus the next morning, I saw Earvin sitting alone on the concrete outside, staring off into space, lost in the deepest, bluest funk you can imagine. I knew for certain that the Lakers had come to a defining moment.

"Isolation is the sum total of wretchedness to man."
—*Thomas Carlyle*

Back in Los Angeles, meanwhile, the front office of Jerry Buss, Jerry West, and Bill Sharman had gotten together. They decided to search for a replacement and then to dismiss Westhead. The team was in a state where a price had to be paid. Something, or someone, had to be purged before trust would return. A terrific coach lost his job as a result. It was nobody's fault, really. It was just a by-product of turmoil, of losing.

On Wednesday, November 18th, after we beat the Utah Jazz on their home court, a bombshell went off as the result of a private meeting between Coach Westhead and Earvin. It does not matter what was said, but immediately afterwards Earvin told reporters that he wanted to be traded.

The next day the ax fell, and Jerry Buss called a late afternoon press conference, announcing a co-coaching system. Jerry West and I were supposed to split the duties. But West really didn't want to coach again. After Buss laid out his plan, West stepped up in front of the reporters and said,

"Naw. Riley's the coach." When I got in front of
the microphones, I just followed my instincts and
said, "I just want to let you know that if nobody
wants this job, I'm happy to take it." And I did. I
wasn't about to let this chance pass by, even
though I hadn't asked for it. Through an accident
of history, I was named interim head coach of the
Los Angeles Lakers.

Before I became a coach, I had spent eighteen
years coming up through the ranks. Among other
things, I was a bench warmer and a role player.
(My sole role when I first joined the Lakers was to
keep Jerry West and Jimmy McMillian in shape.)
The zenith of my pro playing days was as part of
what they called the "Magnificent Seven" of the
1971 Lakers team. After being traded to Phoenix,
I returned to Los Angeles as a color announcer to
Chick Hearn and was even a "traveling secretary"
to the team. I can still remember making flight
arrangements and handing out boarding passes to
players at the departure gate. On the media side,
I was a production assistant who developed story
ideas on the team.

The reason I became an assistant coach was to
gain more knowledge about the subtleties of
coaching so I could convey them in more depth
during a broadcast. First I was an interim assistant
coach when Paul Westhead first took over for Jack
McKinney, then an assistant coach, and then an
interim head coach, and finally coach. That's when
the whole new role descended on me. The stroll
down this career path taught me some very valuable lessons.

Riles' Rules for Triumph from the Trenches

• *First, never demean the time you spend in the trenches.* If you pay attention to what you're doing, you can learn an awful lot about how an organization behaves, and that can be very useful later on.

• *Second, use any time when you aren't on center stage to strengthen your powers of perception.* Even being on the bench or working around the periphery of the Lakers was like attending a master class in professional basketball. It's strictly attitude that lets you learn.

• *Third, keep reminding yourself that attitude is the mother of luck.* When I was named coach, some guys said, "Well, of course, he was at the right place at the right time!" And that's probably true. But, I also know this: There are millions of middle managers in corporate America scared to death that they are going to be picked off in the next reorganization. They're afraid they haven't been promoted fast enough. Or they're worried they've developed "trench stigma" because they've been down there so long. These people are unlikely to be lucky. Not because they've not advanced fast enough. But because they radiate fear, anxiety, and defeat. Luck is literally all how you look at it.

Luckily, my opportunity to step to the forefront came at exactly the moment in time when the players themselves were ready to surrender their negativity in favor of a Core Covenant.

There wasn't much time to wonder what it all meant. The very next day we faced San Antonio again, a division-leading team that had very recently whipped us badly.

For me, the opportunity for leadership had tapped me on the shoulder and said, "It's you, buddy." Everyone dreams of that moment and feels they're ready for promotion. But there's a big difference between being ready and being prepared.

When the opportunity comes, you have to use every resource at hand. My best resource is always my wife, Chris, who had recently completed the demanding studies and training necessary to become a marriage and family counselor. We talked for hours about the stresses within the team and what might be going through the players' heads. We knew that restoring trust was the key to turning around their mental state.

Athletes, especially professionals, are hypersensitive to issues of trust. They've worked hard, expecting to reach a place where justice is uncomplicated: you give effort, go by the rules, produce results, and you'll be okay. Anything that crosses up their faith in this formula—such as conflict with a coach—brings out bitter mistrust. There's a constant tension in the minds of athletes between their wish to trust and their fear of a raw deal lurking in the shadows.

The same is true for everyone, but athletes feel these things in a piercing way. Earlier than most people, outside the protective circle of the family, immersed in the highly charged, hierarchical environment of athletic competition. As early as junior high school, their fortunes depend on the judgment of people they barely know, people whose

"A great manager has a knack for making ballplayers think they are better than they think they are."
—*Reggie Jackson*

emotional and decision-making styles may seem completely foreign.

Chris and I knew instinctively that the stand I needed to take had to be trusting, firm, fair . . . and it had to be taken fast. I walked into my first team meeting as head coach and wrote on the black-board: "A house divided against itself cannot stand. You are either *with* me or you are *against* me."

It was simple. A coach had been dismissed. Positive results were now expected. If they didn't show up, quickly, the players themselves would become the next target. "You are the ones who can turn this situation around," I said. "If you continue to lose and continue not to play as a team, what are people going to say? Obviously, they'll say that the Lakers fired the wrong guy. If that happens, they'll break this team up with trades, ship some of you out of here, and hope to draw a better hand.

"But, if you're really a great basketball team, you're gonna win in spite of me."

I wasn't bluffing. There were no scapegoats left. It was time for resentments and hidden agendas to be let go. They had a clear and fair path to pursue. Drop their selfishness. Put their full efforts behind the team. Create success. And then the chaos would vanish.

Positive Covenants Are Born

   . . . in the depths of crisis,
   . . . when hidden agendas are brought to light,
   . . . after the supply of scapegoats is exhausted,
   . . . if the first seeds of real trust are sown,
   . . . as teammates start acting positively for
     each other,

. . . when the barriers to enthusiasm are
overturned.

Covenants are not born overnight. How long
could the Lakers sustain this renewed flow? That
was still an unknown. Like any new leader, I was
enjoying a honeymoon. I used that time to solidify
relationships with the key players. They, and the
way they act and perform, are the living embodi-
ment of the Core Covenant. Key players are a
coach's bridge to team leadership. When they
come forward and sign the Core Covenant will-
ingly, their positive qualities define the core of the
team.

Riles' Rule of Declaration

There are only two options regarding the commitment to a Core Covenant. You're either IN or you're
OUT. There's no such thing as life in-between.

In this kind of a crisis, a coach must understand
the motivations of the key players. In Kareem's
case, the most persuasive appeal I could make was
to his desire for equanimity. Kareem hates a fren-
zied situation. That's why he had tried to stand
aloof, withdrawn from the unhappiness inside the
team. "Look," I said, "I don't know how long I'm
going to be here. But while I am here, I hope you
understand the situation. This team needs you to
help hold it together." "I'll play for you," Kareem
said. "You don't have to worry about me."

That was all he said, and it was all I needed. He
was *IN*. The situation was much tougher with other
members of the core. Magic, Nixon, and Cooper
were all young, strong-minded, and talented. They

had an intense, almost innocent thirst for instant ego gratification and recognition. Despite being close friends, these needs made them somewhat petty about each other. "You guys are all very young," I said. "You could play ten years together and go down as the greatest trio of guards in the history of the league. You should want to be godfathers to each others' children. That's how tight you ought to be." For a while, at least, they managed it, and perhaps that small vision for the future helped them to do it.

I told the team as a whole that from now on, problems would be communicated and worked out within the circle. We had to behave as a family. No more dirty laundry handed out to the media. We struck a fundamental principle in our new Covenant: no one could be "an anonymous source" and a Laker at the same time.

They responded by winning twelve of their next fourteen games. Scoring, rebounds, and blocked shots were all way up. Off the court, the warmth in their personalities started to reemerge. They were loose and happy, enjoying each others' company. And I started to hear choruses of "Real Love" by the Doobie Brothers echo on our bus rides.

Then, on December 19th, events that began with an injury to Mitch Kupchak proved—even more convincingly—how valuable this still-developing closeness was going to be. Once Kupchak went down, Kurt Rambis, our "Rambo," became a core player and a starter. He was a real talent, and I can still remember his long blond hair flapping down to his shoulders as he moved around the court. But we still needed more insurance. As we looked over the list of possible replacements for Mitch, one guy stood out as being either our salvation or potentially our downfall—a very singular personality named Bob McAdoo.

"Doo," as the players called him, had gone through a rocky series of ups and downs in the NBA. He was Rookie of the Year for 1973, league Most Valuable Player in 1975. For three seasons he averaged more than thirty-two points per game. But—like many high-achieving players on low-achieving teams—he was depicted as always being on the lookout for Number One and got the reputation of having a terrible selfish streak. Starting with his fifth season, he got traded frequently—six times in six years—each time for less and less value. And he was now twenty pounds overweight. A longtime Detroit Piston heckler named Leon fondly pegged him "McAdon't" when Bob played for that team.

I met with the core players, told them who we were considering, and put the question to them: "Is this guy good enough to help us win a championship? Do we want to deal with his alleged idiosyncrasies in our family?" To a man, they all agreed, "He's an incredibly talented player. If he works hard and scores points for us, we can make him a leader."

The players now had the cohesiveness to make a tough, mature decision about team staffing—one that is frankly beyond the capabilities of many sophisticated management teams. Before, a guy like McAdoo would have increased the chaos. Thanks to the team's Covenant, he became the missing piece of the puzzle. He took off the extra pounds and gave us a huge scoring lift off the bench, night after night. Without Mac's scoring, shot-blocking, and rebounding, we would not have won the 1982 championship. I can tell you that the player we signed was a McAdoo.

As a personality, we had not underestimated the total package we were getting in McAdoo. We found out, as soon as he arrived, that he was still a very competitive guy. Whenever someone talked idly in the locker room about an activity they liked, he automatically started bragging about his own great abilities in the same field. Didn't matter if it was shooting pool, making love, or climbing mountains. Before long, the guys coined a phrase: "If *you* do it, 'Doo do it." They ribbed him in the positive way that only emerges when true trust and mutual commitment exist.

Team commitment is exactly what is hanging up employees in American business, and it's one big reason why so many of the workplaces in America have become so dreary and humorless. More than ever, it's clear that teamwork is the key to global competitiveness. But people are hardened by all the downsizing, "right sizing," and destaffing; and they are afraid of acting with commitment—of committing themselves to the company team, because they don't know if the company will commit back to them.

Workers have it worse than pro-basketball players because the rank-and-file don't have fat contracts to protect them. On the other hand, the only successful players in industry *or* in sports are the team players. It's a great gamble to take—to be an all-out team player without knowing if the company can repay the trust by keeping the team strong and growing. However, it's the stellar team companies (such as Levi Strauss and 3M) that have done the best job of avoiding the cutbacks

> "I hold it, that a little rebellion, now and then, is a good thing . . ."
> —*Thomas Jefferson*

> "I have always thought the actions of men the best interpreters of their thoughts."
> —*John Locke*

and offering the surest prospects for job security. And the alternative is worse, because a company without true team play has already lost.

Ultimately, a team belongs to the people who get the job done. The leader exists to serve them, to create an environment in which their talents can flourish, and that is the coach's or leader's obligation to the Covenant. The only way to do that is through communication, and that doesn't just mean words. During playoffs, for example, I have rented pool tables and VCRs with tape libraries and had them set up on security-guarded hotel suite floors. I've had meal buffets catered into restricted banquet rooms. All so that the players wouldn't have to hassle even leaving the hotel on the road. And I've asked staff to go to department stores and buy stacks of regular towels (in *real* colors, including—would you believe?—pink, but not a single standard issue white), so the team members would feel less like they were besieged in their alien hotel rooms. Some people may think that this should be the work of a social director, but for me it's a touch of leadership with a clear goal. And it isn't blackmail or bribery. It's giving the warriors everything that they need to go into battle, because that is what warriors deserve.

"If he works for you, you work for him."
—*Japanese proverb*

There's a fine line between serving and being subservient. Direction and discipline establish that line. You have to know when to push and demand. My time to step up and claim that skill came along in early March of 1982, close to the end of the season. Despite everyone's best intentions, effort levels had begun to slip, affecting overall performance. Suddenly we lost four games in five. A deeply embarrassing showing at home against the (then) lowly Chicago Bulls was the last straw. We had been holding meetings, players had voiced opinions about what we needed to do, but those same players had failed to carry out their own recommendations.

The Winner Within listens to the voice of the team and makes that voice confront reality. Another role of leadership is to be the Enforcer of the Covenant. With the playoffs only a month away, we had to shed our hypocrisy. The Core Covenant had to evolve one final step beyond being an unspoken agreement. We had to make it a clear, conscious contract. And everyone on the team had to decide—would he sign on the bottom line, backing up his commitment with action? Would he consciously declare himself to be *IN* or *OUT?*

We held a team meeting in the last week of March. The topic was Standards and Practices. Everyone was given a chance to speak up. As a group, we detailed exactly what we needed to do to win a championship. Then, the next time we convened as a team, I told them, "Talks are great, but if the things you agree to get applied on the floor, we don't need any more meetings. You as a team have set *standards* that you think will make us a championship team. We as a group will *monitor* each other. And I as your coach will *enforce* them. You might not like the consequences of failing to get behind the team's standards." The team understood and accepted the rightness of our Covenant, and some of them knew that if they stayed *OUT* it might mean *bench.*

This moment transformed me as a coach. I've never changed back. Far more important, this moment prepared the Lakers of the 1980s for an era of significance. I still get goose bumps thinking about it.

The essence of the Core Covenant is totally positive peer pressure. It replaces blaming and finger-pointing—two vicious enemies of teamwork—with mutual monitoring and mutual reinforcement. In a constructive way, it coerces everyone on the team to support each other and the goals of the Covenant.

When in force, leadership knows right away who is with them and who is against them. Borderline performance and clique-joining become untenable. And, it is all enabled by trust.

"Trust is the lubrication that makes it possible for organizations to work."
—*Warren Bennis and Burt Nanus,* Leaders

Riles' Rule on How to Release Covenant Energy

Positive peer pressure intensifies any team's performance and brings it closer to peak. Covenants can be energized only in an atmosphere of total trust. That trust makes honest criticism a sign of confidence and caring.

In the immediate case of the Lakers, Covenant energy drove us right out of the slump and back into our best form. That stepped-up flow of team play gave the coaches enough confidence to introduce another defense to the players. Because it was new, and other teams hadn't had a whole season to scout it and break it down, this new defense was like having a powerful secret weapon.

There are protective defenses and there are destructive defenses. This one, which we called "FIST," was designed to destroy. It relied on our guys covering their basic assignments *and* moving in at the right moment to trap the ball-handler, like the five fingers of a single hand closing into a powerful fist. When we executed it well, FIST totally changed the rhythm of a game. It forced our opponents to play quicker, and to make more mistakes, creating a lot of fast-break opportunities for us.

It was a strategy that could only work through intense cooperation.

The 1982 Lakers also proved how powerful it can be when a core has the luxury of staying together long enough to learn each other's moves and outlast their early mistakes. Their ability to absorb this defense so quickly, so late in the season, equipped the Lakers with a powerful added surprise. After a first-round bye, we swept Phoenix and then San Antonio, winning by an average of more than ten points a game. The finals matchup was against Philadelphia.

"All men can see these tactics whereby I conquer, but what none can see is the strategy out of which victory is evolved."
—*Sun Tzu*

The 76ers had home-court advantage and an appetite for revenge dating back to the 1980 finals.

We struggled a bit through the first half of game one. Then we opened the second half with FIST.

It kicked off a forty-one to nine scoring run, one of the most devastating runs in NBA playoff history, and we beat the 76ers, 124–117. Philadelphia's coaches spent considerable time planning responses to FIST, but we used that defense only 30 percent of the time. As a result, we could switch back to our conventional defense and create more confusion for them. No matter what adjustment they made, we kept blunting their attack—forcing turnovers, running almost at will. Over a twenty-minute stretch of game four, we scored fifty-two points without taking a single shot from distance.

Approaching game six, we led the series three to two, and so had a cushion. I neatly folded a complete change of clothes, from shirt and slacks to sport coat, and locked it inside my briefcase. Why my briefcase and not a garment bag? Because I didn't want to seem presumptuous. But inside, I was totally convinced that we'd be splashing in champagne before the night was over.

Confidence was the theme of the pre-game talk. I began by visualizing the locker room disgrace of last year's Disease-of-Me playoff defeat. My talk then brought them back to that very first day we had assembled with me, as team and coach, how we had decided there were only two choices—to be *with* the team or *against* the team. I reminded them how we had agreed to demand the best from ourselves and from each other.

"This is our day," I said finally. "Everything has worked out perfectly up to this point. We're here, in our city and on our day, to win a championship in front of our families, our friends, and our fans. There is no pressure. All we have to do is take care of business."

We were up by nine to nothing almost immediately, and we held that lead all the way to half time. At the start of the second half, Dr. J began to take the 76ers on his shoulders with a great individual effort. He threw in eight points before we could score at all. But then, midway through the fourth quarter, as he flew down the lane with a chance to take away our lead, McAdoo suddenly loomed up. Reaching from behind he blocked the shot into the hands of a teammate. That set off a fast break, which ended with Kareem dunking at the opposite end of the court.

"You only live once, but if you work it right, once is enough."
—*Joe E. Lewis*

We won going away. As the last ten seconds ticked away, I ran out to the foul line, raised both fists, and took the scene in—knowing it was about to erupt. I wanted to fill my mind with every memory, every impression that it could possibly hold.

Cooper was right behind me, doing the same thing. Guys on the bench had begun jumping around like their legs had turned into pogo sticks. Fans were rushing the floor. Earvin ran to the bench and grabbed Eddie Jordan, while Jim Brewer wrapped his arms around the both of them. Kareem and Norm Nixon got caught up in the press of the crowd, unable to make their way through the sea of humanity.

"Doo"—the former cast-off—finished with three blocks, sixteen points, nine rebounds. Without him we wouldn't have won.

Earvin was named MVP of the series, just as he had been in 1980. This time it wasn't for one extravagant performance; it was for constantly sustained basketball excellence. His line was 13 rebounds, 13 assists, 13 points.

Early in the year, Earvin had been made the villain for Coach Westhead's dismissal. Now things were different. In spite of attendants guarding the locker room door, a middle-aged woman struggled into the middle of the crazed scene in our locker room. She walked over to Earvin while he was absorbed in postgame interviews, leaned over, and spoke directly into his ear. "I was one of the ones who booed you," she said. "I wanted you to know that I'll never boo you again."

No doubt about it: the relationship with the fans had been healed too. All it took was time and the right direction. Because it takes time to erect and enforce the Covenant, patience becomes a powerful virtue. With trust restored, people begin to see patience for what it actually is—an intelligent choice and an indispensable investment. The maddening, distracting, and ultimately destructive focus on selfish ends recedes into the distance. The craving for the immediate "gimme" disappears.

It takes time and maturity to build a Core Covenant, and it must be regularly renewed. Once you've done it, you have created a precondition for success to live to a ripe old age. You're ready to become significant. I believe this is a universal truth, and I was lucky as hell to stumble over it over a decade ago. The power of the Covenant is a principle known by every great business, every significant team, every extraordinary organization in the world.

From citizen to family member, from our job to our membership in a religious congregation, from driving a volunteer fire truck to paddling a whitewater raft down the Colorado, we all play on a number of teams in our life. Each of those teams must be governed by a Core Covenant. You can help bring them into being or share in its renewal. But first *you* have to decide: Are you with the team or are you against it? By embracing the Covenant, *The Winner Within* answers that question without hesitation.

Time-Out

The Disease of Me has claimed real victims, and the team has run out of excuses and scapegoats. It wants to restore the trust and confidence it felt during the Innocent Climb, but knows that the team relationship must now be based on something more thoughtful and solid. This survival need, often sensed in a time of great crisis, is satisfied by a Core Covenant that creates standards to which the team is totally committed. A successful Covenant works only if team leadership constantly upholds and enforces the Covenant's bonding principles.

4

Thunderbolts

"Sweet are the uses of adversity."
—*William Shakespeare*

"Now you're lookin' at a man
that's gettin' kinda mad;
I've had lots of luck, but it's all been bad.
No matter how I struggle and strive
I'll never get out of this world alive."
—*Hank Williams*

August 30th, 1992, Florida City: A young couple walked through rubble where their house used to stand, the same house where the young man had been a boy, where his father had lived for fifteen years. Looking around, they saw ripped-up hunks of aluminum siding from destroyed trailer houses, pink tufts of fiberglass insulation scattered, cracked two-by-fours, and wet, shiny-looking spots in the grass which turned out to be shards of broken glass.

Two framed photographs were the only family possessions they could find. The man looked across all the adjacent home sites, each one as demolished as his own.

"It doesn't look like a town," he said. "The trees are all naked or gone. It's a whole other world."

Because of a natural phenomenon called Hurricane Andrew, the husband and wife who searched their home's wreckage for belongings were among more than a quarter of a million people who were left homeless overnight across a two-hundred-mile-wide swatch of South Florida. Their houses, as well as the shops and businesses where they used to work, were equally swept away.

"People want to know what's going to happen to them," the mayor of Florida City said. "But there is no quick fix." A woman with three children told a reporter, "It hurts to think about the future."

Still, human beings are a lot more resilient than they realize. With the phone lines down, storm survivors communicated by painting messages on the sides of buildings. A spray-can telegram on the side of one house told friends, GRANDMA NEWTON IS OK.

"Life only demands from you the strength that you possess. Only one feat is possible—not to have run away."
—Dag Hammarskjold

Andrew was a disaster greater than most of us will ever experience. The scars it left will be slow to heal. But the people of Florida will build again. They will be back. That's what a Thunderbolt experience should teach you to do: take on adversity and come back, better than before.

A Thunderbolt is something beyond your control, a phenomenon that one day strikes you, your team, your business, your city, even your nation. It rocks you, it blows you into a crater. You have no choice except to take the hit. But you do have a lot of choice about what to do next. That much is in your power. In the coming years, expect the sky to blaze with Thunderbolts. They're part of the game of constant change.

"Success in life comes not from holding a good hand, but in playing a poor hand well."
—Denis Waitley and Rem L. Witt

Our whole planet seems to be a collection of flash points. Only about sixty of the world's one hundred and ninety current states existed at the beginning of the century. Most of the globe's new nations emerged in just the past five decades. In Africa, in Eastern Europe, everywhere—governments and borderlines are changing at accelerating speed. More often than not, those changes are introduced through coups, strife, and bloodletting.

The Winner Within must know how to field the strife-filled change of Thunderbolts—and that includes winners of every sort, because Thunderbolts can strike businesses as easily as they do governments, communities, or individuals. In fact, business columns and magazines are chock-full of Thunderbolt reports every day.

- A two-year-old child dies and as many as 300 people are stricken when a fast-food chain is hit with an outbreak of bacterial poisoning.
- Terrorists sabotage the World Trade Center, exposing thousands of people to great danger, causing multimillion-dollar damage, and disrupting countless businesses.
- Two people die and another becomes seriously ill when, despite three layers of tampering protection, someone puts cyanide in a brand of cold capsules.

Some Thunderbolts are sheer shots out of the blue. Others spring out of partly cloudy skies, where vigilant attention to the weather reports could have provided advance warning. That means monitoring trends, public policy issues, and regulatory agencies.

- In January 1984, AT&T implements the divestiture of its regional subsidiaries decreed by the U.S. Department of Justice—thus shrinking the size of Ma Bell and affecting the destiny of more than a million employees.

• After medical complications are reported, a brand of intrauterine contraceptives is ordered off the market by Federal regulators. The manufacturer ultimately goes bankrupt.

All of these are Thunderbolt situations, and Thunderbolts are a prime factor in upsetting the competitive applecart. Whether it is a powerful competitor drastically lowering its pricing or a quality inspector dramatically increasing standards, a Thunderbolt spells immediate adversity for someone. But that adversity also carries a positive charge: it strips away all the nonessentials and forces you back to your basic strengths. Adversity shoves you down to your core values and beliefs, to the things that matter most. Back on bedrock, you find the reasons and the strength to carry on and carry through.

"Life is not a spectacle or a feast; it is a predicament." —*George Santayana*

Sometimes, when adversity strikes, we rail against fate. We brutally and unfairly punish ourselves or we lash out at the people around us. We blame others. We stop and wait for someone else to show us the way, to open the door. Or we play the victim: "That's the way it goes. There's nothing I could do. It was meant to be."

That's what happened to the Lakers in 1983. We were the defending champions, with yet another chance at becoming the first team to win back-to-back NBA championships since 1969. Then disaster struck.

Our last regular season game was a completely meaningless contest against the Phoenix Suns. We were down to the last few minutes, already plotting playoff strategy. James Worthy, a brilliant twenty-two-year-old rookie who played the game with the same kind of sweet intensity that Marvin Gaye brought to soul music, swooped into the lane to rebound a missed shot. He collided in midair with the Suns' power forward and fell to the floor. At the instant he hit the wood, he heard a bone in his lower leg snap.

I was aghast. James was the top draft pick in the entire league and had been named to the NBA All-Rookie Team. He was scoring for us in double figures. "Why did this have to happen now?" I thought bitterly.

"It is a very bad thing to become accustomed to good luck."
—Publilius Syrus

Still, we had more than enough to win. We advanced to the finals with eight victories against just three losses. But in the very last game prior to the finals, lightning struck again. Bob McAdoo, one of the chief reasons we had won the previous year's title, tore a hamstring muscle and was lost to us. Then, in game one of the finals, our first-string shooting guard, Norm Nixon, suffered a shoulder separation.

Taken together, Worthy, McAdoo, and Nixon had generated 40 percent of the points our team had scored all year. Losing all three destroyed our attitude. We all silently decided that if anyone had the right to lose, it was us. This simply wasn't our year—what else could we do?

Never mind that we still had three of the finest players in the league—Magic Johnson, Kareem Abdul-Jabbar, and Jamaal Wilkes—all in perfect health. Never mind that our bench was strong, and that we were actually ahead in the third quarter in every single game of the finals. Instead of focusing on our remaining strengths and letting them blossom even more, we mentally gave in. We drank in all the solace that our injuries had elicited from fans and media. We assumed that we were off the hook, that the consequences of losing somehow wouldn't fall on our shoulders. With that attitude, it's easy to understand how we lost four straight to the Philadelphia 76ers, one of the few sweeps in NBA finals history.

Riles' Rule of the Primed Pump

After you have invested your total effort in priming the pump, performance seems to flow along effortlessly. But when a Thunderbolt takes away one or two of the key players, the rest of the team must stage an enormous increase in effort to keep the flow of success constant.

Rocked by adversity, people often get so much empathy and caring poured on them that their own misfortune actually starts to feel good . . . sort of special: "What a tough break," everybody tells them. "You don't deserve it." What soothing consolation!

But sympathy is like junk food. It has no real nourishment. The emptiness comes back very quickly. And nothing gets accomplished in the meantime. There is never, really, any release from the consequences of adversity until you decide to do something about them.

Forget about sympathy. Strengthen your state of mind instead. Even if the odds have shifted against you, go after your goal with the same effort, the same belief, and the same faith.

Somewhere in the 1983 finals we made the classic resignation to adversity. We decided: "It's OK. We're not supposed to win." And that decision made us let down even more. When we went into the locker room after the last loss, we all had our heads down for a moment. Then we looked at each other and said, "Hey, it was a good season anyway." The subconscious autosuggestion of blameless defeat.

It took us an entire year to realize what we were doing wrong. If you're going to be a championship team, you have to think championship thoughts. "It's OK to lose" will never be one of them. If you hear yourself, or your teammates, starting sentences with "If only" or "I could've" or "We should've," you've heard thoughts that are going in the wrong direction. After our "Thunderbolts" season, the Lakers of the 1980s developed a standard saying for whenever they heard a teammate make an excuse: "Shoulda, coulda, and woulda won't get it done." And they were right.

Riles' Rule on Beating the Sympathy Syndrome

Giving yourself permission to lose guarantees a loss. If you don't steel yourself to other people's sympathy, you cheat yourself and your team. Shoulda, coulda, and woulda won't get it done. In attacking adversity, only a positive attitude, alertness, and regrouping to basics can launch a comeback.

One thing you learn quickly in the NBA—playing one hundred-and-then-some games a year against the fiercest, most talented athletes available—is that losing is just as much a part of life as winning. It's critical to realize that failure is as much a part of the picture as success. No matter how hard you compete, you ultimately have to absorb losses. So you *do* absorb them, with grace and a determination to learn whatever they might teach. But never be tempted to embrace them.

Be angry. Be upset. Be determined to come back stronger next time. But do not be accepting. People who are negatively conditioned accept defeat. People who are positive don't.

Broken bones, torn muscles, and separated shoulders are simply part of an athlete's life. They are normalcy. Every profession, every area in which people work to do their best, has its own certain kinds of setbacks. Facing those setbacks is what keeps you alive. The most profound opening words to a book I've ever read is the three-word sentence that begins M. Scott Peck's *The Road Less Traveled:* "Life is difficult." Once you realize and accept that fact, you're ready to live life successfully. You find a genuine kind of peace. You focus on controlling all the things that you are able to control. You rededicate your energies to basics.

The most profound basic of all is simple hard work.

The Lakers had plenty of work ahead, on their road to significance. No Thunderbolt—or even three of them—should have shaken us from our vision or master plan.

Sometimes it isn't even the big things that break down a person's will to succeed. Sometimes seemingly minor setbacks cause psychological meltdowns. That surely happened to the Knicks early in the 1992 season, my first one with the team.

It was a time of total change. Our family left behind twenty years' worth of community roots to establish a new home, find new schools and new friends. I was working with new players, staff, and management. They in turn faced an all-new system and team philosophy. Expectations were incredibly high all around. We won five of our eight preseason games, and showed flashes of brilliance that seemed to justify everyone's hopes.

The media were in a state of hyperawareness, ready either to coronate or crucify us, depending on how we opened the regular season. As it turned out, Alfred Hitchcock couldn't have crafted a worse nightmare than our opening: two road losses to expansion teams, both in the same weekend. "The Riley Era Begins," proclaimed the local papers, with cartoons of me being hanged in effigy in Times Square.

"The crisis of yesterday is the joke of tomorrow."
—H. G. Wells

Late on the Sunday night we returned, one of the core Knicks, who had been there before, called me at home. "I ain't gonna make it through this again," he said. "I can't take this anymore. It's going to kill me." Several others took the same attitude. The ghost of old failures had hit them in the face, and they were ready to go into the tank. They were helping to forge a Thunderbolt of negativism where none yet existed.

The people who stayed level-headed were the ones who helped us get back to winning. We regrouped, steadied ourselves, and ended up in the playoffs, throwing a seven-game barn-burner against the World Champion Chicago Bulls.

Those two early losses were just a tiny blip on the radar screen. But, because of timing, they caused some people to lose perspective and to bankrupt suddenly all their fresh, new hopes. Had we kept on believing that way, their worst fears would probably have come true. Psychologists call it the self-fulfilling prophecy. Unconsciously, we try to shape our reality to fit our own preconceptions, even when those preconceptions are self-destructive. And if you're thinking "I expect to fail," or "It's okay to fail, after what happened to me," you'll fail. Simple as that.

Determination conquers every failure. Some people are superstars in absorbing and recovering from Thunderbolts, and even in exploiting them. One of these is surely Lod Cook. A business writer recently began a profile of Lod this way: "If I could choose a mentor, I'd pick Lodwrick (Lod) M. Cook, chairman of the Los Angeles-based Atlantic Richfield Company (ARCO)." It's been my good luck that I've *had* exactly what that writer wished for. Ever since I've known him, Lod Cook has been a tremendous leadership mentor for me.

Lod grew up during the Depression years, in a north Louisiana town called Grand Cane, in the backwaters between Shreveport and Natchitoches. His childhood home was fireplace-heated, hot water came from a kettle on the wood-burning stove, and light from a kerosene lantern. The toilet was a shed out back. His high school graduating class numbered five. But he was born into a supportive, encouraging family, and given a sense of security along with a taste for embracing challenges.

Lod Cook studied to be a mathematician and engineer, but his oil company career began in personnel. This was good judgment on someone's part because Lod's biggest charge comes from working with people—cajoling, pushing, prodding, praising, defining team goals, and letting everyone know how well they're doing. At first he was overzealous, but he gradually learned how to get a wide range of people to a common point by pulling them toward a single goal.

In 1977, while president of Arco's transporta-

"The future belongs to those who believe in the beauty of their dreams."
—*Eleanor Roosevelt*

tion division, Lod served as chairman of the Owners' committee of the Trans-Alaska Pipeline System. This was the largest private construction project ever done. Seven major corporate owners, plus state and federal government overseers and several contractors, all collaborated. The big oil fields at Prudhoe Bay, Alaska, were ready to go. America was in the midst of an oil crisis.

Then a Thunderbolt hit: an already-built pumping station burned down.

"The things which hurt, instruct."
—*Benjamin Franklin*

Most people on the project had extensive pipeline experience. Lod did not. In search of a solution, someone mentioned a new, relatively untested compound called a drag-reducing agent or DRA. They said it might provide greater oil flow through the pipeline with the remaining pump stations. Because it looked like a gluey brand of hair tonic, Lod took to calling the stuff "slickum."

Experienced pipeline engineers laughed the DRA off, but Lod was intrigued. If it did what it was supposed to do, they might not need to build four other pump stations that would otherwise be needed. Lod supported tests in ARCO's labs. They started with a two-inch pipe and found that "slickum" made oil flow more easily with less pumping effort. They tried a bigger one and then a bigger one yet. The results kept on turning up positive.

Scientists still don't know exactly why, but somehow the compound makes oil molecules flow in a straight line—a phenomenon called laminar flow—instead of tumbling randomly along in a state of friction and turbulence and therefore more slowly.

The hard part came after the tests: convincing seven different competing corporations to try an idea their experts doubted would work and feared might damage refinery operations downstream. Experts thought it was a joke. Then came an unforeseen Disease-of-Me problem. The company that made slickum suddenly decided to capitalize on the groundwork Lod had done and jack up their price. Tough negotiating brought them quickly back down to earth.

Engineers had planned the pipeline to carry 1.4 million barrels of oil a day. Slickum increased the capacity to over 2 million barrels. Meanwhile, those extra pumping stations never had to get built. Between reduced construction costs and increased oil flow, hundreds of millions of dollars were saved and gained. The public benefited as much as the companies that built the pipeline. The nation also benefited through reduced oil imports.

A decade later, after he had been elevated to CEO, Lod faced another outsized challenge. In 1989 state and federal legislators were pushing for solutions to California's smog problems through the use of alternative fuels in cars and trucks. They were close to hurling a Thunderbolt by passing laws that would mandate the use of an alcohol-fuel blend called M-85. This change would have required conversion jobs on millions of cars. There would have been tremendous expense and many years before any significant reduction of air pollution. Also, bringing alcohol-fuel blends to market would have cost oil companies a lot of expense and difficulty. Even then the air pollution benefits from M-85 in Southern California would have been questionable.

Leadership at the other oil companies dug in

for a legislative fight. Meanwhile, the *Exxon Valdez* oil spill was very fresh in the public's memory. In a head-to-head battle over reducing pollution, the oil industry might well have looked like villains.

In March of 1989, Lod consulted with top ARCO officers about a crash program to make a cleaner-burning gasoline every bit as effective as M-85. The concept wasn't new, but better computer models were now available for measuring how different gasoline components affected air quality. ARCO's scientists ran their newest research through computers, balanced the possible blends for pollution reduction, then ran tests on the most promising ideas.

By September ARCO stations across Southern California were selling the new gasoline. And, in a spirit of industrywide teamwork, Lod offered ARCO's research results to his competitors. Since then, other companies have brought out reformulated gasolines and ARCO has added a second one to its line in Southern California. And reformulated gasoline has gotten official recognition as a bona fide alternative fuel.

Instead of coming off as environmental spoilers, Lod's company has won top awards from the California Society of Professional Engineers and the South Coast Air Quality Management District, plus high praise from the Natural Resources Defense Council.

Lod wasn't out to win friends, though. He was out to make his company "bolt-proof" to an impending blitz and to prosper in the long run. He did it the same way he handled the pipeline situation—with a decisive move that allowed everyone to win. Reformulated gasolines are one big reason why air quality is actually improving in Los Angeles. At the same time, they've also helped enhance ARCO's position as the state's most innovative and successful gasoline retailer.

"It was as exciting as a major oil discovery for us," Lod says. I think it's even bigger than that. Businesses are like basketball teams. They can only continue to exist if they win. Businesses score through the bottom line. By collecting great profits at the same time they did something good for the environment, Lod and ARCO set one hell of an example for business people. They also drained the juice from a looming Thunderbolt for their own best interests.

Riles' Guide to 'Bolt Proofing

• Stick to your key strengths and core values. They will be your emergency generator when a bolt strikes.
• Ground the 'bolt's shock value by involving your core team.
• Exploit the "equivalent benefit" in any adversity and milk it for as much personal development as you can get. Coming back from a Thunderbolt has little to do with a grand strategy and a great deal to do with strength of heart and the conviction to follow a basic plan.
• And, for God's sake, get the weather report before you go out the door! *Meaning:* Stay attuned to any regulatory hearings, competitive innovations, new twists in behavior or attitude of key teammates, or slippage in standards or procedures that give the inkling a Thunderbolt may be unleashed.

The person who makes a difference, who leads his or her team into significant achievement, will be the one who starts by keeping wins and losses in perspective. You have to take what comes at you, but roar back at it and not let it overwhelm you. Refuse to accept that a Thunderbolt has the power to ruin your life, and that's half the job of overcoming it.

"It ain't what you eat, but the way how you chew it."
—*Delbert McClinton*

Most of us would like to live our lives in a security bubble. But life won't let us do that. Adversities are universal, and sometimes come in a hell of a lot worse form than being outscored in a basketball game or even coming up short on the monthly profit-and-loss statement.

My wife is so close to one of her Los Angeles friends that they're practically sisters. Even the rhythms and phrases of their speech are nearly identical. Very recently, that friend went through something so trying, so excruciating, that no one could possibly have blamed her for giving up in despair. The way this woman handled her Thunderbolt was sheer inspiration for me, and I hope it is for you, too. It was as powerful as any playoff drive and more personal than a heartbeat.

"The softest things in the world overcome the hardest things in the world."
—*Lao-Tzu*

One evening in the first week of March 1992, about the time that Chris and I were ready to sit down to dinner in our Connecticut home with our two children, a long-distance phone call came from their godparents, Steve and Holly Chabre.

Something big had happened in their lives, and they wanted to help the people closest to them understand. Suddenly, the greatest adversity they had ever faced struck them. Holly had breast cancer.

Right now, breast cancer is the greatest killer of women in America. One hundred fifty thousand cases happen every year. Nearly a third will be fatal.

Holly was forty-two when an examination revealed the chilling news. There had been no history of cancer in her family. She didn't smoke. She didn't fit the usual high-risk categories. At her most recent mammogram, though, the doctor had detected a microscopic spot. Surgeons then removed a tiny, crab-shaped mass with a small center and long, radiating arms.

The following Wednesday, the lab tests were due and Steve was the point man for the doctor's call. When Steve arrived home early that afternoon instead of phoning her with the results, Holly realized that it could only mean one thing. She ran out to the driveway and found Steve in tears. She heard herself saying, "I'll be all right, honey. We got it early. I'm going to be fine."

"My only hope lies in my despair."
—*Jean Racine*

Because her other breast also showed some abnormal cells, Holly chose to have both removed. She also elected to undergo an extensive operation that would create new breasts. It meant massive surgery, but Holly entered the hospital in a serene state of mind. She had done everything in her power, including many hours of prayer. Now it was up to the surgeons.

Meanwhile, the morning in April that she entered the hospital in Los Angeles, Chris lay down on our bed in Connecticut, doubled over in sympathetic pain. I'd never seen anything like it.

Holly's combined operations took more than twelve hours. The surgery and the recuperation that followed took so long because tissue—muscle and arteries—were transplanted from other parts of her body. For two weeks she couldn't move her

arms or her upper body. Even the slightest motion
could pull all the transplant work apart. Everything was so difficult and so awful that it became
funny in a macabre way. As the anesthesia wore
off, she felt her bed shaking and rattling. All the
drain tubes coming out of her body were slapping
against the bed's steel rails. The entire floor was
sliding back and forth. She had woken up in the
middle of a massive earthquake!

When the shaking stopped, she saw that her
upper body was riddled with staples. Because it
had been risky for her to remain unconscious for
so long, the surgeons had had to close her up
quickly and fine-tune their work later. With a
nurse's help she called up Chris and joked, "You
should see this. It looks like Freddie Krueger at-
tacked my chest with a staple gun!"

After two weeks of motionlessness, she under-
went six months of intravenous chemotherapy,
which is an ultimate test of anybody's attitude.
Even Holly admitted that it was the most difficult
experience, both physically and emotionally, that
she'd ever been through. She had nausea. She lost
her appetite. All her hair fell away, even her eye-
brows and lashes.

Now, as I write this, the chemotherapy is done.
I can ruffle the new fuzz on top of her head and tell
her it feels like puppy fur. The world stopped for
her for more than half a year. Everything changed.
Even Holly changed, in the sense that she became
even more herself.

Over dinner, celebrating her final chemotherapy
treatment, we told her how inspiring it had been to
watch her handle this Thunderbolt. She in turn
credited Chris and others for helping her through

"The heart's memory eliminates the bad and magnifies the good; and thanks to this artifice we manage to endure the burden of the past."
—*Gabriel Garcia Marquez*

the crisis in ways ranging from finding the best doctors to providing the constant flow of moral support.

"How in the world could I not become a better person," she said, "with all these people doing so much for me? When people care that much, there's nothing you can do except get out there and fight. You have to pick yourself up, dust yourself off, and say 'Let's get this over with!' It takes a year? Okay. What's a year? It's nothing."

She still faces a lifetime of constant alertness, but today Steve and Holly and their teenage daughter, Nicole, are closer than they have ever been. When she talks about the support her friends and her family gave, Holly says, "That was one of the real joys of having cancer."

Not many people would put the words "joy" and "cancer" into a single sentence. Holly is a natural exception. "I wouldn't want anyone to go through this," she says. "But don't feel sorry for me. I'm fine. All it did was strengthen me and my family. I ended up finding out how lucky I was."

We sometimes need adversity to fathom our true depths. Dealing with profound loss can be the most meaningful, most rewarding event in our lives. When your heart is broken, that makes it possible for wonderful things to come inside, and they stick with you after the healing is through.

One day the people in Florida City will know the truth of that statement. Thunderbolts are powerful enough to knock you off your feet. But they are also transitory. Endurance can kick their ass. People like Lod Cook, Holly Chabre, and even the 1983 Los Angeles Lakers provide living proof.

Time-Out

Core Covenant in place, the team is *together* in organization and in attitude. With a far more solid foundation than the Innocent Climb, and healthily beyond the petty bickering of the Disease of Me, the team seems en route to uninterrupted success. But life is never that smooth, and Thunderbolts—unexpected catastrophes beyond your control—are nearly certain to challenge the Covenant and to test the character of the team. Once it's accepted that life offers a steady stream of difficult challenges, *The Winner Within* accepts Thunderbolts will come and focuses on self- and team-discipline and on building a sense of anticipation that minimizes adversity and even extracts benefit from it.

5

The Choke

"There is the greatest practical benefit in making
a few failures early in life."
—*T. H. Huxley*

You probably didn't know this: General
George Custer had plans beyond Little Big
Horn. He was out for the Presidency of the
United States. Everything was going to fall
into place: the fame he earned as the Union's
youngest general in the Civil War had waned over
the years, but he'd get back on top by clearing the
Sioux tribes out of Yellowstone Country. As soon
as Chief Sitting Bull was whipped, a rider would
light out for the nearest telegraph office, sending
word to St. Louis in time for the Democratic
Party's convention. Custer would be swept into the
1876 Presidential nomination. As a military hero
with a fresh victory, he'd trounce the Republicans
as easily as he had conquered the Sioux.

Of course, you know what happened on Custer's
road to the White House. He choked. More than

"God gets you to the
plate, but once you're
there you're on your
own."
—*Ted Williams*

ten thousand Sioux, Cheyenne and Crow, holding more than twenty thousand horses, were gathered for their Great Summer Conference. They had home-court advantage: they knew every ravine and ridge. Custer ignored the numbers his scouts brought in. His troops burned smoky campfires, tipping off their position to the enemy. Instead of verifying if his tactics were justified, Custer simply sent two hundred men into a direct and completely fatal charge.

Choking is the defeat that results from failing to understand or accept the reality of your competitive position versus an opponent. Failing at a critical moment can come from overestimating your strength as easily as from underestimating it. Either case leads to failure at a critical moment of performance allows yourself to be victimized through a myth.

- Custer was a wild-eyed *under*estimator of his enemy's strength.
- In contrast, Japan's MITI (the Ministry of International Trade and Industry) is constantly *over*rated as an enemy and as the mastermind behind Japanese industrial superiority, while it has in fact made a number of pivotal business planning mistakes in the auto industry, and others.
- For decades, experts now concede, the Soviet Union's military capabilities were *over*rated, and that led to enormous Western World defense spending as a result.
- Large manufacturers of computers drastically *under*estimated the potential market for the personal computer. Some forecasters expected that only two hundred thousand would ever be sold, the number now sold every four days!

For most businesses or individuals, these choking seizures are serious but not lethal, as they were for Custer's troops. Still, we all face situations in which we need to keep the Myth Within from strangling *The Winner Within* at a crucial moment. Choking is a universal experience, and choking is always miserable—but by no means necessarily terminal.

"It isn't making mistakes that's critical; it's correcting them and getting on with the principal task."
—*Donald Rumsfeld*

The most important trait of ruling dynasties is that *dynasties don't choke.* By comparison, freezing at the critical moment is what runners-up do best. Because of the luck of the draw, there are plenty of cases in which a number-two team chokes, but one or two of its players may not. The worst fate a winning individual can suffer is to be on a second-best team when a dynasty begins its reign. It guarantees the gifted core players on "number-two" ten solid years of frustration. That's why some players break free of the chokehold by trying to find a way on to the dynasty itself. It's simple: every winning player really wants the *opportunity* to win a championship.

When I would coach the Lakers on the sidelines, opposing players would saunter up to me, sweating during a free throw, and say under their breath, "Is there anything you can do to get me on your team? I can *help*. Ple-e-e-e-ze I gotta get with the Lakers!" The magnetism of the dynasty works in business and government, too, and often brings people out of the top team of one line of business into another, where the chances have even more allure. What drew Louis Gerstner from his job as CEO of RJR Nabisco to become CEO of IBM, if he didn't feel he could keep that industrial dynasty alive and make it truly sparkle again?

Even if you can't maneuver a swing over to a

winning dynasty, choking does not brand you as pathetic or as a permanent loser. It *does* mean that you have something to overcome, a psychological barrier or a lack of preparation, before you can show the world your best work. In fact, choking means that you are at least midway in climbing the steps that lead to ultimate success.

"In war there is no substitute for victory."
—*Douglas MacArthur*

These are lessons that anyone who plans to survive the pressures of the NBA must accept, because at the end of every professional basketball contest there are only two possible states of being: WINNING and MISERY. And, Tuesday night, June 12th, 1984, is still the most vivid example of utter misery that I've ever experienced. It arrived in the final thirteen seconds of game seven of the NBA Finals, against Boston on their home floor.

Only days earlier, the series had been totally within our hands. Then we froze. We made crucial mistakes and blew our advantages. By the time those ultimate seconds were ticking away, all chances of winning were gone.

Play was stopped momentarily for a foul. The Boston Garden crowd was dying to celebrate. The delay of game gave them such a ripple of sweet anxiety that they nearly had heart attacks. The ball was inbounded and quickly shot. It took a long bounce off the rim. We tipped it out to half court, with enough time to fire off one last attempt.

While that final shot was still in flight, bedlam broke loose. Fans mobbed every inch of the floor, forcing us to struggle through them to reach our locker room. The nicer people just elbowed past us as they scrambled to touch their heroes. The creeps in the crowd punched and jabbed at us and spewed ugly words in our faces. In the stands, Laker family members were being treated just as brutally. My wife's mother was shoved over a railing.

There was no solace in the hollow hell of our filthy Boston Garden locker room. We could only sit there, wet, stripped down, staring at a floor strewn with towels, tape spools, and paper cups, while the celebration sounds coming from the Celtics' room rumbled through the walls. Earvin Johnson and Michael Cooper sat side by side in complete stillness. Tears were streaming down both sides of Earvin's face.

> ### Riles' Rule on Finishing Without Being Finished
> You have no choice about how you lose, but you *do* have a choice about how you come back and prepare to win again.

We boarded our team bus within the bowels of the building and rode through a tunnel, then down a wooden ramp leading away from the stadium. At the bottom of the ramp, about a hundred Boston fans had been transformed into an ugly mob by their excitement—and by Celtic management's failure to put security where it was obviously needed. Some of them massed directly in our path. As the driver rolled cautiously forward, they began to act like a baboon pack driving off an invader, throwing rocks, bricks, and bottles, smashing the windows of the bus. As the bus slowly rolled along, the mob enveloped it and began rocking it from side to side. Someone grabbed the driver's outside mirror and ripped it away from its mountings. With that, the driver panicked and we lurched forward. The mob scattered and we made our escape.

"To appreciate heaven well, 'tis good for a man to have some fifteen minutes of hell."
—*Will Carleton*

We felt bad enough about choking away the finals. Now Beantown demanded that we run a gauntlet, too.

One afternoon in the following summer, as I was attending a coaching clinic taught by the University of Indiana basketball coach Bobby Knight, he said, "Anytime you have some problems, this will give you a few things to think about."

The book he recommended was *The Art of War*, written by Sun Tzu, a Chinese military commander who'd lived near the time of Confucius. It's the earliest known study of warfare, and after twenty-five centuries, *The Art of War* still influences new generations. Napoleon read it. Mao Zedong used its advice to expel Chiang Kai-shek's larger, better-supplied armies to the island of Taiwan. Afterward, Mao wrote: "We must not belittle the saying in the book of Sun Wu Tzu, the great military expert of ancient China, 'Know your enemy and know yourself and you can fight a hundred battles without disaster.' "

Use knowledge and keep your cool is Sun Tzu's message. His advice stands right up there with "Be not afraid of sudden fear," from the Book of Proverbs, as the two best anti-Choke quotes I know. It was really Chris's mother, Dorothy Rodstrom, who unlocked the power of the Bible for me as a source of wisdom in the fight against Thunderbolts, Chokes, and other adversities. For both Chris and myself, Dorothy has always been the mentor of our family's spiritual life. She's a very caring woman, and she learned teamwork as a registered nurse in intensive care surgery at the age of eighteen. My own mother, Mary, and Dorothy are perhaps the two wisest people we know.

Whenever we've been tested in our life—in basketball or in anything else—Dorothy has trained us to use the Bible as a problem-solving tool. If you're challenged and you just don't know how to get beyond it, look for the underlying problem. It could be arrogance, greed, fear, you name it. Scripture can help explain the source of Chokes and how to overcome them, and that goes for *any* scripture: the Bible, the Talmud, the Koran, the Confucian Analects . . . any of the great Good Books. Most Choke situations are variations on a classic theme. Hey, Goliath, after all, was just somebody else's Boston Celtics . . . until David devised an offense he couldn't handle.

"Let no man's heart fail because of him [Goliath]."
—*First Book of Samuel*

Over- or underestimating your competitor leads to clutching because *you don't know your enemy.* It's just as bad when *you don't know yourself.* First, a lack of self-confidence will prevent you from testing or developing your skills to their fullest: you go through life with a self-imposed performance cap. Second, if you blindly take on challenges beyond your level of preparation, you saddle yourself and your teammates with avoidable disappointment, and sometimes worse. Players have approached me time after time, and said the same thing: "Coach, I'm ready to step up."

I look them in the eye and say, "No, you're not."

"Why?"

"Because you're not prepared."

I love the hunger and the willingness in that kind of player's attitude, but I need to coach them one step more, so that they understand the work they must still invest.

Riles' Rule of Total Preparation

Being ready isn't enough. You have to be prepared for a promotion or any other significant change. Preparation demands mental and physical conditioning and conscious planning. A player who is just ready and *not* totally prepared simply increases risk and is a liability to the team.

Here's an example of how an entire team wasn't prepared. Management didn't realize how dramatic the transition would be when the New Orleans Jazz became the Utah Jazz in the 1979–1980 season. Utah didn't accept the team—even though it was Utah's first major league sports franchise. It's not that Salt Lake City didn't have a lot of sophisticated sports fans: lifestyle differences, and a commitment to a different kind of basketball, built a barrier.

New York Knicks president Dave Checketts spent six and a half years running the Utah Jazz, and he recalled for me: "Salt Lake City was a troubled franchise that had been transferred from New Orleans. They kept the same colors and the same name. What could be a more dissonant combo than Utah and *jazz?* The franchise had traded two first round picks, one of which turned out to be Magic Johnson and had sold Dominique Wilkins to Atlanta for a mere million dollars."

"Success generally depends on knowing how long it takes to succeed."
—*Montesquieu*

When he joined the franchise, Dave studied the marketplace and focused in on two major issues. First, he confirmed that Utah was a very young marketplace, with great quality-of-life pride but relatively low per-capita income. So he had to develop specific fan motivations that would lead to stronger season ticket sales for the market. Then

Dave analyzed the competitive force fields created by four major universities within an hour's drive of each other, all of which had great basketball programs.

He decided to build the season ticket base by showing the fans that the Jazz was not a threat to the college basketball programs. The Jazz set up a new annual summer league that pitted local college players against Jazz team hopefuls. "The fans could see our talent base was much better than that of the college teams," Dave said. "While the fans were coming to see their college teams, they were really being educated on NBA standards and quality. At the same time, the whole concept strengthened our own relations with the colleges. We also started the Jazz Youth Leagues, which today involve fifty thousand kids wearing Jazz Youth T-shirts in a summer basketball program."

Today the Jazz is accepted by the entire Utah community through an ingenious community relations program that invited Utah to welcome the Jazz—by educating and reassuring the fans fully.

When you meet a challenge fully prepared, your effort flows seamlessly. There is concentration and exertion, but no straining. When you go after a goal and you're not prepared, you soon find yourself pressing. The harder you try, the less effective you become. The less effective, the more discouraged—until there is finally an iron-clad conviction that you will fail. Poor preparation is an enemy of free-breathing performance and an invitation to choking.

In the history of the Lakers, there had to be seven disasters before we learned not to choke big games against Boston, before we were totally pre-

"If at first you don't succeed, you are running about average."
—*M. H. Alderson*

pared to be the championship team we could be. Talk about slow learners! Sometimes the victory was so close, and yet the final result was so cruel, that people really started to believe that supernatural forces were at work.

- In the 1962 finals, we came down to a tie in the final three seconds of game seven. We had Frank Selvey, one of the best shooters on the team, wide open in the corner. He missed. The game went to overtime and we lost by three points.
- In the 1963 finals, we actually scored the most points overall, but the Celtics scored when it counted, won more games, and took home the rings.
- In 1966 we lost the first three finals games, then rallied to win the next three. Our momentum exhausted itself at the end of game seven, which we lost by a single bucket.
- In 1969 we swept the first two games of the finals and were poised at three games apiece. We held home court advantage in game seven. Everyone was so sure of a home win that the ceiling of the Forum was rigged with thousands of balloons, to be released at the moment of victory. Instead, the only thing to come down was a Don Nelson shot in the closing seconds. With the score tied and only a fraction of a second remaining, it clanged off the rim, bounced straight up, and then fell through at the buzzer.

Why did the Celtics always get so lucky, right when it counted, and we just plain missed? Was there really an invisible leprechaun perched on the rim, swatting our shots away?

By now, the Celtic Choke was being spliced into

the Laker genetic code. When Jerry West, one of the greatest Lakers of all time, wrote an autobiography in the early 1970s, prior to the first L.A. Lakers championship season, he confessed that he'd started believing it was his fate never to win a championship. It's a testament to Jerry's greatness that he went on to prove his own fears wrong.

Repeated choking is the essence of defeatism. Losing becomes part of your identity. You begin playing to avoid a loss, rather than playing to score a win. The more fearful you get, the more likely it is that your predicted disaster will ultimately come true.

Riles' Rules for Home-Made Misery

- Tell yourself you never had a chance.
- Fear losing so much that you become overprotective.
- Take any simple mistake you make as proof of how fundamentally stupid you are.
- Let the spirit to retaliate against bad luck or flagrant fouls dominate over a sensible plan to win.
- Save your most dramatic choking performances for decisive moments—so that you convince yourself and everyone else that you were born to choke.

Here's how the Lakers created their own misery in 1984.

Late on Friday night, May 25th, 1984, we won the Western Conference Championship, beating Phoenix on their court. We touched down in Boston eighteen hours later, near five o'clock on Saturday evening. Game one of the 1984 finals was scheduled to start early on Sunday afternoon. The league wanted prime television exposure; our fatigue wasn't a priority concern.

Our players had just enough time for dinner and a brief meeting, but no time for practice or special preparation, as they faced the most important part of the entire season.

"Nowhere to go but out, nowhere to come but back."
—*Benjamin Franklin King, Jr.*

Meanwhile, the Celtics had been resting at home for five days. There was only one thing that could happen: we were going to get killed. We had no shot. It was the kind of game you can lose and not feel bad about.

So, with no pressure in our minds, our guys just played hard and let their game flow. We didn't overprepare. No paralysis by analysis. As a result, we beat Boston on their own home floor, 115–109. Figuring we were already dead, we didn't consciously choke.

Nobody had expected the win, least of all us. All of a sudden we had an incredible opportunity in our hands. By controlling game two, we'd have the Celtics in a deep hole. The next pair of games was scheduled for our home floor. A four-game sweep that would unhinge the Celtic Myth looked possible.

Game two came down to its last sixteen seconds. We held a two-point lead, but Kevin McHale had just drawn two foul shots. Since Kevin was 85 percent effective from the free-throw line, I expected him to sink them both and tie the score. He missed the first shot, but I was sure that he would make the second, and I made a big concentration error by not paying attention to the second miss—mulling over the substitutions I might make instead.

To everyone's great surprise, Kevin choked both

shots. Magic got the ball into his own hands and was ready to attack immediately, flying by instinct, before the Celtics' defense could jell. At the very least, we would have forced Boston to foul. Instead of allowing that to happen, *I* choked. Signaling a time-out, I set up an inbounds play. And I substituted a rookie, Byron Scott, in place of an All-Star veteran forward, Jamaal Wilkes, figuring that we needed a ball-handling guard to keep possession away from Boston. I was being overprotective. I focused on the fear of losing instead of the desire to win. What I did in that game is classic choking. It reminded me of something I read once, the worst act of excess caution in the American Civil War, when the Union general McClellan instilled a fear of improvisation in his officers. He sat on one side of the Potomac with two hundred thousand well-fed and well-outfitted troops. Across the river in Virginia was an opposing force of sixty thousand men—many of them sick and poorly equipped. McClellan could have crushed them but wouldn't move. He was playing not to lose instead of going for the win.

Finally, under pressure from President Lincoln, McClellan sent two units against the Confederates at Ball's Bluff. After months of waiting and of suppressing their fighting instincts, McClellan's officers faltered. The Confederates won a small but psychologically important victory. It convinced McClellan to keep on being cautious, right up to the day Lincoln fired him. With proper confidence in his team, McClellan could have shortened the Civil War by years. But he choked.

"In order to win you must be prepared to lose sometime. And leave one or two cards showing."
—*Van Morrison*

> ### *Riles' Rule for Dialing 911*
> What the Heimlich Maneuver is for choking people, the 911 Rule is to choking organizations:
>
> • Clear your mouthpiece of alien debris, all that crap about being destined to lose.
> • Confirm your own vital signs and restore faith in your own basic ability to perform.
> • Search out and destroy the root causes of excess nervous energy and overprotectiveness—sure symptoms that a Choke is under way.
> • Never forget that the misery of defeat is always worse than the misery of the Choke.

After my McClellan-like time-out and substitution of Byron Scott for Jamaal Wilkes, Earvin in-bounded the ball to James Worthy. As expected, the guy guarding Earvin switched over to double-team James, who was then supposed to fire a re-turn pass to Earvin. With the open floor that would create, Earvin would be all alone and ready to attack the defense.

One thing every player learns, early in his bas-ketball life, is to never, ever, throw a crosscourt pass in the back court. A crosscourt pass leaves the ball hanging out in space, with a defender on one side and your own basket downcourt on the other. If that defender anticipates your pass, there's no way to stop the guy from running it in for two uncontested points. But James was then a young player, a second-year man facing his first finals competition. When the second defender ap-plied pressure, James got rattled. He looked away from Earvin, across the court to Byron. If he had been a player with veteran judgment, Byron would have run toward James, meeting the ball. Instead, he kept going in the opposite direction. My view was in a direct line as James whipped the ball toward Byron, across a huge gulf. I can still see the seams of the ball rotating toward me, as if in slow motion, like a car wreck about to happen.

Meanwhile, Gerald Henderson, who had over a hundred steals notched on his belt that year, had been laying in wait for a chance like this. He made a lunge for the ball, deflected it downcourt, and streaked in for a basket that tied the score. Game two went into overtime, where we lost it by just two points. Ghosts of bygone Chokes reared to life again.

Choking not only postpones victory. It also inflicts psychological wounds along the way. In spite of the battlefield freeze that threw away game two, the 1984 Lakers still held terrific position. The series moved to our home court. Two wins there would bring us within one victory of a championship. But losing game two because of a playground-level mistake punctured our confidence. We identified with our one big mistake instead of with our proven ability to play great basketball. We began performing to an imaginary limit. Our fatalistic belief that it was the destiny of the Lakers to gag on the doorstep of success took hold once more. And that's exactly how things unfolded.

"The minute you start talking about what you're going to do if you lose, you have lost."
—George Shultz

This is a lesson that every team and every would-be winner must learn from Day One: you don't back into great achievements, whether it's winning World Championships or busting sales records. You have to approach every potential great achievement in a state of total confidence.

Confidence helped us kick the hell out of the Celtics in game three, 137–104. Then, in game four, we gave in again to the choking mentality.

We had a solid ten-point lead in that game when Kurt Rambis, one of the best-liked, hardest-working players we had, went up to score a basket. Kevin McHale, in the guise of playing defense, but with the intention of winning a championship, clotheslined him and sent him sprawling. It was a blatant take-out, not a simple foul. Our trainer, Gary Vitti, rushed out and ministered to Kurt while we all strained to see if Rambis would get up. It was a foul that might have ended his career. According to the rules, the officials could have ejected McHale from the game, but in big games that doesn't happen.* Instead, they let Kurt shoot two foul shots—as soon as he was able to begin breathing again.

That combination punch of foul and injustice changed the whole mentality of the series. We clicked into a mental retaliation mode and lost track of basketball for the rest of the game. We let the desire to get even dictate our style. We intended to deal out pain in equivalent measure and get away with it, instead of focusing on putting the leather ball through the iron hoop.

All the Celtics had to do was sit back and play basketball. They collected their win in overtime, 129–125.

This Choke came from not remembering who the enemy was. These were the Celtics. We should have been ready for a low blow. We should have been prepared to shrug off dirty play, reject the

"Mounted raiders with iron weapons . . ."
—*The Concise Columbia Encyclopedia*, on defining the Celts

---

*Of course, if the New York Knicks lay a finger on anybody these days, they're candidates for a suspension!

temptations of a get-even, victimized mentality, and keep playing the game.

The Lakers weren't sunk yet. The series was now a 2–2 tie. Whoever won game five would likely win the championship.

Friday, June 8th, the date of game five, turned out to be one of the hottest, most humid days in Boston history. In preparing for that day, we thought about a lot of things—ball movement, hard fouls, what to expect from the referees—but we didn't think about the weather. The Celtics knew it was going to be well over a hundred degrees, with humidity around 95 percent. They brought in air conditioners and powerful electric fans for their locker room. They supplied each player with three fresh uniforms. They ordered hundreds of pounds of extra ice so their players could grab a chilled towel any time there was a break in the action. They told their players to come to the arena in comfortable summer clothes, while I had our guys in suits and ties.

That day's game went down in history as "the Steambath." There was a big thermometer mounted in one corner of the Garden. The television camera crews were showing it almost as often as they showed the scoreboard or the clock.

Within three minutes, my navy blue suit was soaking through with sweat. Before long, salt marks were showing all through the suit. Out on the court, one of the officials keeled over and had to be revived. The Lakers were wilting, too. Our locker room at half time was more stifling than the arena itself. We had no fresh uniforms to change into, no extra ice, no air conditioning or fans to provide relief.

Instead of working out strategy, we spent our fifteen-minute break taking cold showers.

Riles' Rule on Intelligence-Gathering

In any competitive situation, a chief duty of leadership is to minimize the impact of unexpected conditions and distractions on the team in combat. This demands the trained eye, awareness, and judgment of the leader if the troops are to prevail on the battlefield.

I was like a military commander who hadn't taken the time to study the lay of the land—which is part of knowing your enemy. The Steambath turned into an eighteen-point victory for the team that had prepared itself right—and that was our opponent.

Game six was a cushion game for the Celtics. Byron Scott got a great shooting streak going and we pulled out a win. Once again, the series was tied. Then we came into game seven prepared with everything—air conditioners, extra uniforms, ice chests. I even blew out circuit breakers in the ancient arena as a result. But it was too late. I remember the guys coming in to practice on the morning of the game, showing signs of nervous energy—talking too fast, keeping the "unbeatable" myth alive, focusing on the fact that we had never beaten the Celtics in a seventh game.

The Celtics came in loose and confident. We almost knew that the seventh game was theirs. As Cedric Maxwell walked out of their locker room, he told his teammates, "Get on my back. I'll carry you." He did, with twenty-seven points. Boston outrebounded us, outmuscled us, outsmarted us through every minute of the game. They deserved the win.

Then came our scene of ultimate choker's misery and our bus ride through hell. It was awful, but it was not worse than the lingering misery of the summer and pre-season to come. We all knew that we had to shake the choker image. If not, the team would surely have gotten dismantled. Management was already wondering who to trade, what new pieces to bring in.

If anyone predicted then that the 1984 Lakers would not only hold together, they would also go on to dominate the decade, asylum attendants might have locked that person away. But we eventually proved that choking can be overcome.

Can there be any value to the experience of choking? Yes. For us it came in realizing, finally, that the historic barrier we kept tripping over, the Celtic Myth, existed only in our minds and imaginations. From being labeled chokers, from having enough salt rubbed in our wounds, we drew the motivation to work harder, coach smarter, prepare better, and to let go of the Myth. One year later we got the job done, once and for all. We never again lost to the Celtics in finals competition.

"By indignities men come to dignities."
—Francis Bacon

Choking can make you want to give up. Or it can be the ultimate prod to do your best. You make the difference. How do you react when you choke? Are you determined to overrule the Choke reflex and to take your team beyond it?

Time-Out

After being hammered by Thunderbolts, the team feels both discouraged and victimized, while it hungers to recapture the solidity of the Covenant and the success rush it once knew in its Innocent Climb. But, things have yet to hit the bottom of the Choke. Caution, fear of further failure, and an exaggeration of opponent strength or weakness all distort the team's perception of reality. Like the Disease of Me, the Choke is self-induced; but the Choke stems from poor preparation and low self-confidence rather than greed or resentment. The Choke can only be overcome through a total overhaul of attitudes.

6

The Breakthrough

"Men die of fright and live of confidence."
—*Thoreau*

Sometimes you have a feeling that you're about to embark on the most important trip of your life. When this feeling hits you, all of a sudden you understand your purpose. The clarity of what you must achieve is overwhelming, and you have the first confident inklings of what must be done and, maybe, even how to do it. That's how I felt right before game two of the 1985 NBA Finals, the single most important game the Lakers played during the eighties.

I imagine it's also exactly how a Vietnam veteran named Jan Scruggs felt on the night he innocently went out to see a movie and what he saw on the screen changed his life forever.

A breakthrough is a positive Thunderbolt. It enables the team and The Winner Within *to grasp*

"Great works are
performed not by
strength but by
perseverance."
—*Samuel Johnson*

*and to realize their mission by defining and
fulfilling the most important performance goals
in life.*

Jan C. Scruggs, a man destined for a breakthrough
rendezvous, began life as a small-town boy from
Bowie, Maryland. Barely a year out of high school,
he and the rest of his squad from the 199th Light
Infantry Brigade were pinned down all night long
by North Vietnamese machine-gun fire. Scruggs
should have died that night, but one of his buddies
stood up and purposely drew the fire to himself,
buying the rest of the squad a few seconds' chance
to retreat and survive.

By May 28th, 1969, when Scruggs took serious
shrapnel wounds, over half of the men in his company were either dead or wounded. He was sent
back home to Bowie at a time when antiwar feelings split the hearts of American people more than
anything had since the Civil War. Scruggs walked
the street wearing his uniform, and people he'd
grown up with booed him. And when he read the
papers, he saw that politicians were distancing
themselves from the war as fast as their speech-
writers could carry them. Instead of glory or recognition, Vietnam veterans were left to nurse their
spiritual wounds and to reconstruct their attitude
toward life.

"I have fought a good
fight, I have finished
my course, I have
kept the faith."
—*II Timothy, 4:7*

Meanwhile, Scruggs had to face choices about
what to do with the rest of his life. He drifted
aimlessly for a while, then slowly put together the
money and the resolve it would take to enter the
local community college.

Up to this point his story is similar to those of
thousands of other young men and women. They
made a choice, while still in their teens, to do what

their country asked of them. They were shipped to a remote country. They fought and survived treacherous conditions. They went out on reconnaissance patrols with living friends and returned to base carrying dead bodies. Then they came back home, sometimes missing a hand or part of a leg, sometimes carrying shrapnel, and found that their sacrifices didn't matter. Instead of a Breakthrough to look forward to, not a few saw life as a dead end.

Leading Indicators of a Breakthrough About to Happen

• The frustration of knowing great sacrifice, but having that sacrifice unrecognized,
• Deep loneliness, but still a compelling need and desire to act on the behalf of others,
• A hunger to reclaim dignity for oneself and one's teammates after rejection or failure,
• An unflinching recognition that core healing must take place,
• A team leadership that acknowledges it may have been wrong or ineffective, so that others can withstand criticism and challenges more easily.

Can you compare what happens to a basketball team with what happened to the people who served in Vietnam? Matched up against real warfare, what we do in the NBA is nothing but play-acting. When we say "Do or die," it's just a figure of speech. Scruggs and the other veterans of that war know those words as a precise code of survival.

But in another sense there's a tremendous equivalency in everyone's life experiences. Jan

Scruggs was wounded in spirit. He was having trouble finding an aim in life and, at the same time, he grieved about a situation and wanted to set it right. These were his worst and loneliest moments; but such moments can set the stage for your best. It happens when you search within yourself for strength, when you stand firm and make a point about who you are and what you believe in.

The Lakers were wounded in 1984. You might almost say they were wounded by their own hand. If you're a competitor, you have to learn to tolerate getting beaten. But you can never tolerate beating yourself, and self-defeat is the inevitable destiny of the choker.

". . . [I]n ourselves are triumph and defeat."
—Longfellow

We were dominating the Celtics in the 1984 finals. We thrashed them in game one, on their home floor. We beat them by thirty-three points in game three. We were ahead by ten points in game four and cruising, then it all changed instantaneously with that statement foul against Kurt Rambis. We changed our attitude from warrior to victim.

Two days after losing the deciding seventh game of the 1984 finals, we were back in Los Angeles for our last team meeting of the season. I looked at their long faces and said, "There's only one thing we're going to play for next year. I want you to think about this all summer. Even though we lost, they can't take away our pride or our dignity, we own those. We are not chokers or losers. We are champions who simply lost a championship."

We came back sharply focused. All year long we heard about how we were the "showtime" team that folded as soon as things got tough. Even Larry Bird called us chokers. The Celtics and their fans referred to us fondly as the L.A. Fakers. Abuse and sarcasm were heaped on, and we just kept taking it. We had to. But we steadily achieved a tremendous sixty-two-win season and ripped through the first three rounds of the playoffs with eleven wins and only two losses. Finally, on May 27th, 1985, we got back to face our tormentor once again, the Celtics, in Boston Garden.

Wavering on the verge of Breakthrough, we still had to navigate through one last disgraceful defeat. The next day's headlines called game one of the 1985 finals THE MEMORIAL DAY MASSACRE. A 148–114 humiliation that wasn't even as close as the score suggested. It was the most embarrassing game in the history of the Laker franchise. It was our ugliest nightmare coming true, on national television no less. At the moment of truth, we saw ourselves become exactly what we had been called: Choke artists, underachievers, pansies. Even their reserves outplayed our first team. Scott Wedman, a journeyman, came off the bench to shoot eleven for eleven, right in our faces. "Why is it," I wondered, "that every time we play the Celtics we get paralyzed with this fear, while they become stronger?"

As the humiliation grew along with the score, you could see our guys quit. Something dramatic happened within the Celtics after the Massacre. They became strangely compassionate, not the surly, arrogant, killer-instinct thugs that they had been the year before. They talked respectfully about us to the media after the game, in spite of having stomped us into a vat like a winemaker crushes grapes. Maybe they had come to the same conclusion about us that we had ourselves: we were just a sparring partner the gods had provided on the way to another title. No sense being brutal.

"Even the knowledge of my own fallibility cannot keep me from making mistakes. Only when I fall do I get up again."
—*Vincent Van Gogh*

Then we had a space of time, the three days until game two, to pull ourselves back together, just like Jan Scruggs had time in between his tour of Vietnam duty and when he began to build the foundation of his Breakthrough.

Scruggs did well enough at the community college to transfer to American University in nearby Washington, D.C., and earned a master's degree in psychology and counseling. His life was on track, but his memory was still seared with images of friends who died in Vietnam. America wanted to forget the war, but Scruggs knew intuitively that the war experience had to be healed, not forgotten. He dreamed of a memorial for the men and women who gave their lives, but he also realized his limitations. He was just a college student. There was no organization behind him, he didn't have money. He couldn't see how he could ever get such a job done.

In 1979 he went to see *The Deer Hunter*, Michael Cimino's powerful movie about the impact of Vietnam on a group of small-town friends. Robert De Niro, Christopher Walken, and John Savage on screen could have been Jan and his hometown high school friends. In the movie, one of the heroes is crippled, one is destroyed, and the third fights to save them both. All of them, and even the friends and sweethearts they left behind, are changed in ways that they can't even comprehend. Yet, in spite of all their pain, at the end of the movie the survivors somehow find themselves singing "God Bless America."

Scruggs couldn't sleep after seeing that movie. One day in Vietnam he had witnessed incoming mortar fire blast twelve of his men, ripping their skulls and their bodies open, spreading their in-

"Let a beauty full of healing and a strength of final clenching be the pulsing in our spirits and our blood."
—*Margaret Abigail Walker*

sides across the terrain. Those images came back fresh. Again, he wasn't alone. All across the country, suicide hot-line phones were ringing, and counselors found themselves talking to ex-soldiers who had seen *The Deer Hunter* and had found their minds flooded with painful memories no longer suppressed.

On the morning after he saw that movie, Scruggs told his wife that he was going to build a memorial to the Vietnam War dead. Not a memorial to glorify the war, but a testament to the people who gave their lives. They would never be forgotten again. All of their names would be there. It would happen soon, not decades down the road, because it was needed now, to ease the nation's suffering and to help heal the wounds.

As the Memorial Day Massacre ended, I remember walking off that parquet floor, catching the knowing looks on the faces of the writers at the scorer's table, then going down the tunnel and into the wretched bowels of Boston Garden on the way to the locker room. For the first few minutes, I just stood there in misery. From the looks on the players' faces, I knew that they didn't believe they could beat this team. I didn't believe it either, at that moment. Finally I got this much out: "I don't have anything to say. But I will tomorrow. We'll meet at ten o'clock."

The other coaches and I spent a long time hopelessly wondering what we could do. We looked at the tape until midnight, until I finally identified a course of action. Even though it's a team game, a basketball team relies on its superstars to be superstars. I was going to land on the most glorious player in the history of the NBA, the leader of the team, knowing that he would take it on behalf of

"Duty cannot exist without faith."
—*Benjamin Disraeli*

the team and enable them to lift their own expectations.

In the midst of several subpar performances, Kareem's was the worst. He was listless. McHale and Robert Parish were beating him down the court and scoring practically at will. Kareem was a thirty-six-year-old warrior, maybe his age was a problem. The reporters sure thought so. In the morning, every paper in the country centered their story on how Kareem Abdul-Jabbar had looked out of it, uncompetitive, a millstone on the rest of the team. It was some of the worst commentary that I ever read about a great player.

We pulled twenty or thirty sequences out of the game tape and edited them into a single string of embarrassing performances, most of them featuring Kareem. Other players played poorly, but I had to zero in on the captain. And if he could take it, the whole team could come together stronger than before.

We set up twelve metal folding chairs, a VCR, and a monitor in the meeting room the next morning. Kareem had been through a million team meetings in his career, and he had long ago developed a habit of sitting in the back. But when I walked in, ten minutes before the meeting time, he was sitting alone in the front row. His elbows were jammed against his knees and his hands propped up his chin. He was staring at the monitor, watching the game tape by himself. The other players came in, saw the captain acting differently than they were used to, and they quietly went to the back rows. They sensed that sparks would be flying.

For nearly half an hour, in analyzing the game and reviewing the footage, Kareem was the target.

"A strong and well-constituted man digests his experiences (deeds and misdeeds all included) just as he digests his meats, even when he has some tough morsels to swallow."
—*Friedrich Nietzsche*

All he did was listen to me, watch the edited tape, and say, "You're right, you're right. I didn't jump. I didn't get back. You're right. I was terrible." As I watched him, I got the eerie feeling that this was exactly the treatment he both wanted and needed.

Kareem was demonstrating something about greatness in a player. The truly great ones can take it. Not just from the opponent, but also from their coaches, from the press and the fans. Kareem was strengthening the team's backbone in the way that he took the criticism. He knew that the more I could target him, the stronger his teammates would become.

For the next three days we worked on transition drills, because we had gotten beaten by not playing an intense transition game. We devised some excruciating, physically demanding drills, and focused relentlessly on them for most of our practice time.

> "The only place where success comes before work is in the dictionary."
> —*Vidal Sassoon*

On the second day I looked at Kareem and was concerned that he was overworking himself to purge his role in the defeat. "I should rest this guy. He isn't as young as everybody else. I'm going to run him into the ground," I thought. So I slid over next to him and said, "Kareem, take a break. I think you ought to sit down and rest."

"F——— rest," he answered. "I don't need a break."

Jan Scruggs must have gotten the same feeling after addressing a meeting of Vietnam veterans in Washington. He took the plan public, and he got the same failure messages from them that he had been getting from other people: it wouldn't work, politicians wouldn't vote any funds for anything connected to Vietnam. But afterward, a veteran named Robert Doubek, a lawyer who had served in the Air Force, came up to Scruggs and handed him a key idea. If he would form a nonprofit organization, a Vietnam Veterans' Memorial Fund, any contributions towards planning, designing, and building the monument would be tax-free. Doubek also gave Scruggs his support and counsel over the next months. Using his own money, Scruggs filed the necessary papers, got the Fund registered, then held a press conference on May 28th, 1979, ten years after a mortar round had exploded and sent him back to America.

Scruggs was now doing the basic legwork that underpins any victory. It still reminds me of our 1985 remedial drill marathon in the playoff series. I liked what I had seen in our drills, but I was still troubled about what to say to the team before the game. I spent three days polishing my final comments to the team before we went out on the floor. As we concluded our shoot-around on the morning of the game, I told the players to be on the team bus by six o'clock. And this time, unlike most times, we were going to go alone. No reporters, no family, no friends, just us.

We went back to the hotel and rested, then I came down to the bus half an hour before it was supposed to leave. Everybody else came early, too, except for Kareem. By ten of six they were all there, sitting in complete quiet. You could hear people breathing.

At half a minute to six, Kareem still hadn't arrived. I wondered what was up, and whether I'd have to fine the captain at a moment like this.

Then I saw Kareem running up to the bus, with another man sort of straggling behind. It was his father, whom all the players and coaches fondly called Big Al. Kareem swung up onto the bus and asked, "Can my father go to the game with me?"

I said yes. I knew that I was breaking the standard, but I also knew that Kareem wanted his father there. I could relate to that. They got on the bus together, sat down in the back, and I could hear them chatting. And then it hit me. Maybe he knew it. Maybe not. But Kareem had brought me our message, too. Thanks to Big Al and the voices of all fathers like him, I now knew what the Lakers needed to hear.

Sometimes, when you need to inspire people, all you have to do is pay attention. They will inspire you with the insight of how to inspire *them.* This, for me, was one of those times.

Jan Scruggs, too, learned how infectious inspiration can be. Wire services carried his story into newspapers all across the country. Veterans and parents who had lost children to the war effort wrote him hundreds of letters, expressing every emotion from joy to anguish to outright bitterness. The money they sent in, though, wasn't enough. This was going to take millions more.

Then John Wheeler volunteered to help. He was another veteran, and his emotions had been stirred when he read about Scruggs' goal. Wheeler was also a graduate of Harvard Business School, Yale Law School, and West Point. He knew powerful people in several professions, and he used his contacts to build a tremendous volunteer force of fund-raisers, publicists, and friends in high places. By July of 1980 a bill had passed both houses of Congress and had been signed by President Carter, setting aside a space next to the Lincoln Memorial and allowing the Fund five years to raise money for

"How often things occur by mere chance which we dared not even hope for."
—*Terence*

"The wise and moral man shines like a fire on a hilltop. . . ."
—*The Pali Canon*

construction. Scruggs, Doubek, and Wheeler didn't want to wait that long. Their timetable was for Veteran's Day in 1982.

Watching Big Al and Kareem in the team bus, I sensed they too understood the urgency of their moment now in Boston. My mind began to race back. My father had died more than ten years before I became what he had been, a coach. Along with my mom and five brothers and sisters, I had followed him from town to town, packed into a '47 Woody station wagon, pursuing his dreams. There were a few times during the eighties, maybe half a dozen in all, when I heard his voice, or distinctly recalled his image, at a crucial moment. Each time that voice, that image of my dad had a great influence on me. And I knew now that this was the time to talk about Lee Riley and what he had taught me. This was not about the Celtics, not about X's and O's. This was about Big Al, Lee Riley, and all the other positive voices we have heard in the past.

Riles' Rule of the Leading Voice

When a Breakthrough arrives, there will generally be some message, some voice, that captures the essence of the work to be done. It could be a movie, a novel, a song, a speech, or a sentence rich in images . . . Or, perhaps, Three Wise Men following a star in the sky. Whatever it may be, it is more than just a Sign. These are the *marching orders* that people remember. To energize a team to break through to its goal, some message must ignite that energy.

When we got into the dingy pit that Boston Garden management calls a locker room, there were no television cameras. We made sure that they weren't there. Newspaper writers approached the players for interviews, but they all got the cold shoulder. Big Al sat next to Kareem as he put his gear on, then he left and we went through our final preparations.

It's a beautiful moment when you know the team is just sitting there, waiting to take in something special. They'd heard my voice before, until they were sick of it. But there was no eye-rolling today. They were open, ready to listen and to believe.

Every now and then you have your back pushed up against a wall—that proverbial wall. Yes, it's real. It seems there's nobody you can depend on but yourself. That's how the Lakers felt about facing this showdown. If we lost, the Choke reputation would be chiseled into stone, a permanent verdict. If we won, we had the opportunity to prove that we could keep on winning. We weren't facing machine-gun fire, but, by warrior/athlete standards, it was a do-or-die situation.

I faced Kareem directly and said, "I've known you since we played against each other in high school. When I saw you and your father on the bus today, it made me realize what this whole moment is about. You spent a lot of time with Big Al today. Maybe you needed that voice. Maybe each and every one of us in this room needs to hear that kind of a voice right now, the voice of your dad, the voice of a teacher, the voice of somebody in the past who was there when you didn't think you could get the job done.

"I know there's a lot of you in here who probably don't think you can win today. A lot of you don't think you can beat the Celtics. And it's been proven. The record is undeniable.

"I want each and every one of you to close your eyes. Just sit back and listen." And they did. I had their total, undivided attention.

I started to talk to them about my past and my father. When I was nine years old, my dad told my brothers, Lee and Lenny, to take me down to Lincoln Heights and to get me involved in the basketball games. They would throw me into a game and I would get pushed, shoved, and beat up. Day after day, I ran home crying and hid in the garage. I didn't want anything to do with basketball.

This went on for two or three weeks. One night I didn't come to the dinner table, so my dad got up and walked out to the garage, where he found me hunkered down in a corner. He picked me up, put his arm around me, dusted me off, and then he walked me into the kitchen. My brother Lee was upset with him. "Why do you make us take him down there? He doesn't want to play. He's too young."

My father stood up and, staring at Lee, said, "I want you to take him down there because I want you to teach him not to be afraid. That there should be no fear. Teach him that competition brings out the very best and the very worst in us. Right now it's bringing out the worst, but if he sticks with it, it's going to bring out the best." He then looked at his nine-year-old, teary-eyed son and said, "Pat, you have to go back there."

And I told the players, "I thought I was never going to be able to get over being hurt and afraid, but I eventually did get over it. And before too long, I was sending other kids home to their garages to lick *their* wounds. That's what competition is about. That's what the Celtics and Boston Garden are offering up today."

"It's a little like wrestling a gorilla. You don't quit when you're tired—you quit when the gorilla is tired."
—*Robert Strauss*

I told them of a time I saw my father in 1970. It was at my wedding. He and my mom were leaving the reception and we were about to start our honeymoon. He and I had been talking all day about my career. I had just been cut by the San Diego Rockets. The Portland Trailblazers, another expansion club, had invited me and twenty-nine other players to their training camp. That looked like my last shot. I was $5,000 in debt, and I was about to take on the responsibilities of marriage. It was a great day. But I needed a voice.

As his car was driving away, my father yelled at me, "Pat!" His arm came out first, gesturing, then his head. I began to chase after the slow-moving car to hear. "Just remember what I taught you. There will come a time. And when that time comes, you go out there and kick somebody's ass. This is that time, Pat." Every now and then there comes a day where someplace, sometime, you simply have to plant your feet, stand firm and make a point about who you are and what you believe in.

I told them that I did not realize as the car pulled away, that those were the last words I would hear my father say. He died soon afterward. It was his message that I gave the Lakers that day. It came from the heart. It was inspired by Kareem Abdul-Jabbar and his father and how they connected with each other.

As I was relating this moment, I was slowly pacing back and forth and staring at the ceiling, locked into the image of my father's face. When I looked back at the players, Cooper was crying. A couple of other guys looked like they were about to start. The talk was affecting the team not unlike *The Deer Hunter* had struck Jan Scruggs. Both messages had provided a Leading Voice.

"I don't know what it's going to take for us to win tonight," I said. "But I do believe that we're going to go out there like warriors and that would make our fathers proud."

We went out and won the game, 109–102, which sounds close, but it really was no contest. Through its entire course, I never had any fears about losing. We were always in control. Anytime the Celtics tried to assert themselves, Kareem was right there: thirty-seven points, nineteen rebounds, six blocked shots. A brilliant performance, a complete reversal, a 100 percent return to his best form. After the game, when reporters came around, Kareem got in the last word: "Contrary to public opinion, the demise of Kareem Abdul-Jabbar was greatly exaggerated."

We won three of the next four games, and the 1985 championship became ours. Seven times in Laker history the NBA Finals had been lost to those adversaries. Now the Celtic Myth was slain and the choke image with it.

During the off-season, Michael Cooper told me that the pre-game message had gone so deep for him that the score was already five to nothing before the game started. For those who don't know, Cooper had a grievous leg wound as a little boy, an ugly cut through muscle tissue. Doctors didn't think he'd ever walk right again, let alone become an athlete. He was sustained through those times by a wonderful mother and devoted uncles. So he heard voices from his most profound inner reaches.

"What the inner voice says will not disappoint the hoping soul."
—*Friedrich Schiller*

All of us have at least one great voice deep inside. People are products of their environments. A lucky few are born into situations in which positive messages abound. Others grow up hearing too many messages of fear and failure, which they must block out, so the positive can be heard. But the positive and courageous voice will always emerge, somewhere, sometime, for all of us. Listen for it, and your Breakthroughs will come.

When Jan Scruggs made his objective come true, he helped an entire nation surpass its limits. On November 13th, 1982, Veteran's Day, he was able to watch dedication services performed for the Vietnam Veterans Memorial. He walked the length of the wall, where more than fifty-eight thousand war dead are individually memorialized. The high rollers had donated, the stars of politics and show business had thrown in their support, but most of the millions had come in modest amounts, twenty dollars or less, from Americans of average means, people like himself. People who, like Scruggs and like the Lakers, planted their feet, stood firm, and made a point about who they were and what they believed in.

Breakthroughs happen in every aspect of life, but business Breakthroughs are more likely to come from the head than the heart. Often they entail defining old problems in new ways, or the road to fresh solutions wouldn't even *occur* to you. "There is an old saying," writes McKinsey consultant Kenichi Ohmae in the *Harvard Business Review*, "that to a man with a hammer, all problems look like nails." How rich is your tool kit? Ohmae goes on to ask. How willing—I would add—are you to stretch your mind and to listen to the seasoned voice of your own intuition?

The Breakthroughs in business may be more calculated and considerably less exhilarating than what happened to Jan Scruggs or the Los Angeles Lakers, but they are the milestones that achieve industrial competition, save jobs, and keep the tax base liquid. Who can say that isn't exciting? After all, the fear of losing one's livelihood is probably the number-one anxiety gnawing at most of America today.

All great Breakthrough messages deny the crippling power of fear. Fear of failure will lead you toward despair, wrong decisions, and incomplete performance. It's one of the last hurdles between any person, or any team, and their greatness. Listening to the voice that counsels courage, that affirms your life and your ability will put you in position to do your best. When your back is against the wall, what inner voices will remind you that you've faced down fear before? Whether on a playground, a parquet floor, in a boardroom or on a battlefield: who is the Voice Within who can remind you that courage is your birthright?

Time-Out

Gasping for breath and fumbling for the future while snared in the coils of the Choke, *The Winner Within* will suddenly identify the myths and delusions that are strangling performance and potential. This realization—the Breakthrough—is a positive sort of mental Thunderbolt. The Breakthrough enables the team to grasp its mission and to undertake the most important performance goals in life. The Breakthrough can be achieved only if the team's core is revitalized and if it is challenged to new heights of performance and awareness. Breakthroughs often hearken back to earlier pivotal moments in a person's life and then enlarge them into broader, more important lessons.

7

Complacency

"Each success only buys an admission ticket to
a more difficult problem."
—*Henry Kissinger*

C omplacency is the last hurdle any winner,
any team must overcome before attaining
potential greatness. Complacency is the
Success Disease: it takes root when you're
feeling good about who you are and what you've
achieved.

In the sports business, there may be no better
example of complacency than what is going on (or
not going on) in major league baseball. It was all
spelled out for me one day by my attorney, Ed
Hookstratten, one of the savviest sports media experts in the business. A few years ago, he noted,
baseball was able to negotiate a huge contract for
television broadcast rights, thus giving them a
comfortable excuse to sit back and *not* solve one
of the most serious problems in the sport: the

patchwork makeup of the various team divisions, which has long been overdue for a realignment.

Why should this be such a big deal? Because even major league sports are fundamentally regional. Some athletes are exceptions. Larry Bird, Patrick Ewing, Earvin Johnson, Michael Jordan, Joe Montana—they're known everywhere—but by and large sport celebrityhood is regional. There are media-perfect superstars in Kansas City, Cleveland, and other big cities, but you can walk them down the street in San Francisco and nobody knows who they are. Major media cities also play a role. The stars who end up as fixtures on the national stage are those who couple extraordinary media charisma with outstanding athletic skill. In marketing terms, you could put it this way: there are national brands and there are local brands. What baseball may be overlooking is how to develop the power of its local brands.

Baseball is very short of team rivalries, which is critical, since those rivalries are personified by local heroes. And if celebrities are regional, rivalries are even more so. "For the Los Angeles Dodgers to be in the same division as the Atlanta Braves is ridiculous," Ed pointed out with exasperation. "Look at the way the country is laid out! Follow those geographical lines!"

"Facts do not cease to be because they are ignored."
—*Aldous Huxley*

This outdated organization loses plenty of marketing opportunities. Fans cannot relate to season competition that doesn't have a regional structure. What you have today is a big tangled maze created by old expansion agreements often decades old. "The owners have not created geographic rivalries," Ed went on. "Their ballparks are seeing empty days. They have lost regional competition, which would generate greater revenues. They have also permitted cable-access teams to cross America in competition for fans and viewers, thus injuring local markets. They should be set up to have a series of LCS regional playoff games." Not only would a reorganization sharpen fan and media interest in the game, "it would cut down tremendously on travel expenses, which have risen dramatically in the last several years." Ed thinks that major league baseball owners have been mesmerized by the national television contracts of the past. "There's one more year to go," he forecasts, "and then there will be an avalanche" downward in the value of broadcast rights.

I have no doubt that the baseball owners are shrewd enough to see that a future reorganization is unavoidable, but—if Ed is right—they will pay a costly price for not having done it sooner.

What I say next may sound like a basketball chauvinist sounding off, but the NBA has been just the opposite of baseball. It has been a model of *non*complacent behavior.

Under the leadership of David Stern, the NBA has become the standard for professionally managed team sports. Stern is now recognized as the most astute commissioner in any pro sport. His noncomplacent attitude is always far ahead of potential problems. He is constantly fixing it before it's broke.

Just twelve years ago, retail sales of NBA licensed products were about $10 million. This year they'll be almost $2 billion. The market value of a single NBA team today is bigger than the yearly revenues taken in by the entire league in the early eighties. The game that clinched our first championship of the eighties, game six against the Philadelphia 76ers, wasn't even shown on live television. Due to a CBS decision, Earvin Johnson's greatest single-game performance was seen, via tape delay, at 11:30 P.M. Today every game of the finals is a prime-time centerpiece. From "NBA Today" on ESPN to "Inside Stuff" on NBC, a constant hum of media presence reaches out beyond the games like a magnet. And there are rich story lines for the fans to follow: organizationally, the NBA's divisions are set up as four regional North-South corridors, with clear territorial rivalries.

The NBA is state-of-the-art today. It wasn't always that way. Not too many years ago, the most *un*together team in the NBA was the owners themselves. Nearly three quarters of all NBA teams lost money year after year. Between 1980 and 1981 alone, attendance dropped by 450,000 fans, even with exciting new stars like Larry Bird and Earvin "Magic" Johnson. The league was sitting on top of a lot of value, but wasn't turning that value into revenue.

So certain things began to happen. The franchises realized that unless they partnered up on the big issues, their complacency would guarantee a slide off the cliff. And it all began with some very tough personnel management decisions in the early eighties.

The 1983 bargaining agreement that exchanged the team salary cap for a player stake in gross revenues made the league more "equal" in its competition. Suddenly some teams—the ones that had infinite bucks—had to knuckle down under a spending ceiling. Other teams, who were the poor cousins, had a standard toward which they had to lift themselves. With the salary issue resolved, the owners could then strengthen the business structures of the franchises so that the *human* assets could be managed for a greater return. The salary cap—"cap management"—became a management tool in running the franchises and improved their financial planning capability.

The stake in revenues also made the players happy. The pie got bigger every year. It made the fans happy. NBA contests have more overall consistency today; a TV viewer can generally expect to see solid entertainment, no matter what the matchup.

In addition, the wage cap quelled the public outcry that salaries themselves were getting out of hand. The just previously completed antidrug agreement nixed another public misconception about professional basketball off the court. And the league was on its way. Then it became a simple question of squeezing the marketing opportunities that had always been there in ways that wouldn't conflict with the game. That's one reason, for example (I must confess to my own personal dismay), why *every* NBA locker room is open to the media up to forty-five minutes before, and then again ten minutes after, every game. It's also why the league makes sophisticated media training available to every rookie.

Industrial America may still believe that the core cure for American competitiveness is constantly to take an ax to expenses, through nonstop downsizing. I can remember when the NBA headquarters had a staff of forty. Today, it employs four hundred! And nearly all of the additions were made to seize positive opportunities, not to solve problems.

"If you don't do it excellently, don't do it at all. Because if it's not excellent, it won't be profitable or fun, and if you're not in business for fun or profit, what the hell are you doing there?"
—*Robert Townsend*

None of this would have happened unless the owners hadn't got religion and traded in *Me-think* for *League-think*. Now, you hear some of the baseball execs say, "Hey, we've got to up the visibility of individual players to the level they have in basketball." Maybe. But, alone it's not enough. Generally, just banking on one or two isolated measures outside of a total program fails. It's the "let's try this today" groping of a legend leaning back on its laurels and trying halfheartedly.

Riles' Rule for Kicking the Complacent Ass

Avoiding the solution of a tough, miserable, volatile problem is not discretion. It is cowardice. And it is robbery. Because as long as a serious problem goes unsolved, no team, no person can exploit its full potential. Any coach who doesn't kick the complacent ass on his team will end up kicking his own before long.

The temptation to slack off starts when you're feeling good about who you are and what you've achieved. After you have spent yourself emotionally and physically to achieve the great dream, it's so easy to accept the illusion that your struggle is ended. The congratulations of your friends and family—and maybe even the media—all help you believe that you will stay high on the pinnacle, right where you belong. You've arrived. And it feels so great to let go of yesterday's hunger and insecurity. From that enticing moment forward, it gets harder and harder to make sacrifices.

That's why wise worry is good: not a paralyzing worry, but a healthy awareness of reality. It roots out budding self-satisfaction. While you're celebrating success, someone else is laying plans to move up in the world, and you better know it.

In the early stages, self-satisfaction is very hard to detect. When symptoms begin to show, most people decide subconsciously to look the other way. They don't want their feelings of contentment and fulfillment to vanish.

A team that has just reached a milestone is in danger. When you have momentum, when competitors are intimidated by your accomplishments, it's sometimes possible to give a halfhearted effort and still succeed. A psychology of entitlement is a looming threat. The top spot now belongs to you. The wins will be automatic. The rewards will never stop.

"There is an enormous number of managers who have retired on the job."
—*Peter Drucker*

> ## Riles' Rule of Entitlement
> When a milestone is conquered, the subtle erosion called entitlement begins its consuming grind. The team regards its greatness as a trait and a right. Halfhearted effort becomes habit and saps a champion's strength. Players who feel entitled to greatness should cherish their memories, tend to their pension, and read retirement brochures. Because that's all the future can offer them.

Take a look at the competition between the U.S. and Japan, a topic discussed briefly in the first chapter. At the end of World War II, American industries began some incredible years of prosperity. The mighty American industrial machine made a smooth transition from war to peace. With rationing over and thousands upon thousands of soldiers returning and starting families, there was enormous pent-up demand.

As other nations healed their war wounds, they bought what we made. It was simply the best in the world. No one could challenge our mass-production muscle. Then, having been on the top of the heap for so long, we began allowing a stagnated mind-set to whip us. We got used to cheap, disposable goods—everything from cars to clothes.

Because so many people could afford to get rid of their cars in a year or two, quality and durability gradually became back-burner issues. We just didn't feel motivated to improve. At the same time, firms in other nations—such as those in Japan and Europe—were slowly retooling their factories with the most advanced equipment. Much more importantly, they were retooling their outlooks.

"Men's faults do seldom to themselves appear."
—*Shakespeare*

The recovering industrialized nations saw their openings. The Japanese embraced the thinking of the American Dr. W. Edwards Deming. Deming had strong beliefs about the best way for a business to be organized—with a deep respect for quality, total attention to the needs of the consumer, a commitment to continual improvement, and a supportive attitude toward the people who get the job done.

Deming was a prophet without honor in his own land, while in Japan his message went straight to the heart. The Japanese government started handing out Deming medals for quality to top-performing firms. In 1960 Emperor Hirohito honored Deming himself with a royal medal for spurring the country's industrial rebirth. Twenty years later, the Japanese auto industry produced 11 million cars to become the worldwide leader.

I still remember back in 1972, when I was a Laker player and we were in the midst of our great thirty-three-game win streak, reading a *Los Angeles Times* article one morning over coffee. In it, experts predicted that Japan's recent rise in the electronics field was just about over. There weren't any new products coming along—the videotape recorder idea didn't look practical—so the bubble was going to deflate. And the balance-of-trade deficit, the first one in modern U.S. history, was just a temporary phenomenon.

Discounting an emerging industrial opponent's early wins, we gave them permission ultimately to kick our asses. Fortunately, it looks like we're having some recent success in fighting back. Japanese carmakers are starting to have market problems in the States. Mostly we've learned that you can't go up against principles such as total quality or continuous improvement and win.

The Crime Scene of Complacency

• Tampering with the work ethic as though it were an on-off light switch.
• Hoarding stockpiles of effort for big moments, only then to find the reserves pilfered or drained.
• Sabotaging the quest for a fresh dream.
• Littering performance with "garbage time" rather than pursuing Breakthroughs.
• Looting past glories by leaning on old ways to win.

Complacency is the last hurdle standing between any team and its potential greatness. One moment frozen in time symbolized forever how the Lakers were victimized by indifference and lethargy: the sight of Michael Cooper's rail-thin body lying stretched out on the Forum floor, with his hands over his eyes in a futile attempt to shut out everything that had just happened. The date was

May 21st, 1986. Cooper and the rest of the 1985–1986 Lakers were cut down by our own hand.

Complacency gets its first foothold because some moments in life are so wonderful that we never want them to end. That was how we all felt on the Lakers, knowing that our 1985 finals win over Boston had ended a long era of struggle.

But, as soon as we let wresting a championship from the Celtics define us, we set the stage for a downfall because we failed to dream a new and greater dream. Being "the guys who beat the Celtics for the championship" was whipping a Choke, not a retirement party from the future.

Early in the Lakers' 1985–1986 season, *Sports Illustrated* voiced its opinion that we were perhaps the best pro-basketball team of all time.

For a while we seemed to be proving them right. We got off to the finest start in team history, winning nineteen games of our first twenty-one. If we could have held that pace for the rest of the season, we would have eclipsed the 1972 Lakers' NBA record for regular-season wins. But our first loss gave clear evidence of the kind of trouble that we were going to meet down the road.

November 4th, 1985, was our first home game of the 1985–1986 season. We faced the Cleveland Cavaliers. They had won far less than half their games the year before, and they looked even weaker heading into the current season.

Traditionally, a team gets its championship rings in a pre-game presentation ceremony at their first home game. In the locker room, beforehand, I talked to the players about what the moment meant. I wanted to light a fire under them. In seventeen years, no NBA team had won two championships in a row. I wanted these guys to reach that milestone and addressed the core directly.

"These rings are a symbol of the greatness we showed last year," I said. "But can we reach for something higher?"

"Coach," one of our leaders replied, "we whipped Boston in their own building. We turned *them* into the chokers. How do you expect us to top what we did last year?"

Months later we got taught a simple truth: any-time you stop striving to get better, you're bound to get worse. There's no such thing in life as simply holding on to what you've got.

Cleveland's players endured our half-hour-long ceremony: 17,505 fans congratulated us from the bottoms of their hearts. Each Laker took a slow walk from the sideline to center court under a spotlight. Each one accepted a handshake, then lifted their new diamond-studded championship ring to show the crowd—as the cheers grew even louder.

As soon as that celebration was over and the ball was put in play, the lowly Cleveland Cavaliers kicked our championship asses. They were headed that year for the twenty-first position in a twenty-three-team league, but we found a way to motivate them to a giant-killing performance. Even if we couldn't motivate our own selves.

When the Lakers faced the Cavaliers for the second time in 1985, on December 21st, we didn't let them shame us again. We reeled off a thirty-nine-point third quarter and won going away. George Karl, the Cavs' coach, said afterward, "They are the best basketball team ever to play the game. You have to be smarter than Magic and

"The world is full of willing people, some willing to work, the others willing to let them."
—*Robert Frost*

Kareem to beat these Lakers, and I don't know if that's possible."

Two months into the season, we led the league in scoring. Our wins came by an average of fourteen points per game. We had the best record in the league, nine and a half games ahead of the next-best team in our own division. Then we got another warning signal, another wake-up call. An ugly string of losses began to pile up. Most of them were to teams that we should have beaten with ease.

This is what happens to teams who dream about the past. They go along, seeming okay on the surface, then the bottom suddenly falls out of their performance. After each apparent recovery, the team will cycle back again and again, each time to a worse disaster.

Trying to exhort the team to raise its effort level, I leaned on them during a mid-December practice. One veteran on the team responded: "I only got so much use left in my legs, and I'm not going to use it up in practice. I'm a game player."

He had been a great player, but he was allowing himself to be lulled by a very popular, very wrong-headed notion.

Riles' Rule on Game Players

A classic game player is a fraud. Sloughing off in practice and workouts kills conditioning, invites the Thunderbolt of injury, and ensures game-losing fatigue. A "game player" is committing a flagrant foul against the team's work ethic and its Covenant.

Being a game player is a fiction some people use to excuse themselves from working as hard as they should. People who think they are game players are what coaches call "floaters." They float along on a cushion of talent or of sheer physical size and strength. They don't see what all the fuss over concentration and work ethic is about—until players of lesser talent start scoring in their face, quarter after quarter, simply because they are more in tune with their own game. Floaters ultimately become victims of their own talent. *The Winner Within* simply wants to be known as "a player," without any qualifying term—like "legend" or "superstar"—attached. When NBA insiders call someone a player, they mean that person brings purposeful intensity to every aspect of the game. A true player is a worker, and the term *player* is one of the highest compliments a peer or a coach can bestow.

Eventually, every team has to learn that excellence isn't a destination. It's a process that must be continually improved, just as the Japanese view quality to be. Writing in *The Wall Street Journal*, Peter Drucker describes how a company has to pry itself out of the strategic mud when a business goes stale. "It requires stopping saying 'we know' and instead saying 'let's ask.'"

Maybe we weren't asking all the right questions yet, but at least it was beginning to occur to us that some questions needed asking. We got back on track in early January, winning six out of seven games. After we beat the Clippers on the night of the 17th, the *L.A. Times* sports section ran a companion story about our on-again, off-again effort levels. The headline was ON LAKERS, GARBAGE TIME IS PILING HIGH. In basketball slang, "garbage time" is when there's still time on the clock, but it's already obvious who will win the game. It's a phrase I've never liked. *The Winner Within* knows that every second of a competition is meaningful.

Beneath that headline it said: "Amid the Sweet Smell of Success Is a Danger of Boredom Setting In." One of our key players, asked why he poured on the effort only if we were in danger of losing, grinned and replied, "See me in March." Meaning that he would save himself for playoff time, when the effort really counted.

"You have to perform at a consistently higher level than others. That's the mark of a true professional."
—*Joe Paterno*

Believing it can turn its work ethic off and on at will, the complacent team one day meets a challenge from an unexpected quarter. You try to flick the "on" switch. What do you do if that switch won't respond?

On January 19th, against the sub-.500 Detroit Pistons, we played haphazard defense in the first half, fell behind eleven points, and then tried to roar back. We had it tied with six seconds to go. The Pistons inbounded to Kelly Tripucka. James Worthy lunged for a steal and got one hand on the ball, but Tripucka held his grip and sank a three-pointer to win.

On the morning of the game, both Detroit papers had run stories about how we were possibly the best pro team of all time. But now we were only one game ahead of the Celtics. Three days later we were no longer ahead of them at all. They burned us, 100–95. Within three more days were added two more losses to the record. All of a sudden, "the greatest team ever" dropped four games out of five.

> ### Riles' Rule of the Brilliant Loss
> When a great team loses through complacency, it will constantly search for new and more intricate explanations to explain away defeat. After a while it becomes more innovative in thinking up how to lose than thinking up how to win.

The challenge of competition always involves finding new ways to win. If your company makes a great product, you can be sure that other companies will do everything they can to adapt its best features. Then you will have to win a production-efficiency game, or a cost-containment game, or a distribution game, in order to give yourself the opportunity of winning a price game. The process puts you in the habit of finding new ways to win. When the heat comes on—whether it's the play-offs or the need to come up with a hot new product line—that habit pulls you through.

When the 1986 playoffs arrived, the fact that our attitude had wavered in and out of focus all year made us think more about our entitlements than on new ways to win. Boston had five more regular-season wins than we did. They were positioned for home-court advantage all the way through. We set our sights on meeting them and winning in spite of that disadvantage. After all, we had made four consecutive trips to the finals. We thought it was only natural to be there once again.

The force of our stored-up competitiveness hit San Antonio in the first round. We blew them out in three games, outscoring them by an average of more than thirty points. Then we ripped into Dallas, winning our first game by fourteen. Somehow, though, the second win proved harder to come by. Our margin was only four. Then they beat us two games in a row, each time by a single bucket. A corner of our minds still believed things should automatically fall our way, and two defeats in a row didn't seem fair. It wasn't supposed to be this hard. A team that had scarcely won half of its games had the defending world champions in a 2–2 series tie.

We finally closed Dallas out two games later, on Thursday, May 8th. That left us one day to travel before facing Houston on Saturday for the opening game of the Western Conference Finals, our fifth playoff game in a single week.

We pulled out a twelve-point win. Three more and we would again be up against Boston, where we belonged.

But fatigue was written in all our players' faces. Those who thought their effort levels would kick in for the playoffs suddenly realized that they were running on empty. The holding back during the regular season had put us out of playoff condition. Playing below their potential had become an ingrained habit. The "on" switch wasn't connected.

Game two was scheduled for Tuesday, so we had a little cushion. I decided to cancel Sunday's practice. "You guys go to the beach," I said. "Get some rest."

I don't know what beaches our guys went to on Sunday, but when Monday morning's practice began, they looked like they were still walking in sand. The most listless practice I'd ever seen in my life was a prelude to a public shaming. We went on to give one of the lowest-energy playoff performances of the decade.

Hakeem Olajuwon, meanwhile, came out ready

"He who stops being better stops being good."
—*Oliver Cromwell*

to deliver perhaps the greatest series of his life. He was furious, like a rampaging force of nature. His energy lifted and inspired the Rockets to whip us in three straight games and take a 3–1 series lead. We had to win game five or die.

Fifteen seconds can be a long time in an NBA game, especially when they turn into the final seconds of a season. Late in game five against Houston we still had a chance to turn our championship drive around. Near the fifteen-second mark, Earvin Johnson hit a baseline jumper for a three-point lead. All we had to do was play smart defense and hold on for the win.

Coming out of a time-out, the Rockets set up a three-pointer for their point guard, Robert Reid. His shot careened off the rim and into James Worthy's hands, but then it somehow slipped away before James got a solid grasp. Mitchell Wiggins snagged the loose ball for Houston and fed it to Reid, still standing behind the three-point line. I knew he wouldn't miss it the second time.

With the score now tied, we ran the clock down to its final seconds. Our strategy was to win it on one shot. Failing that, we would have a five-minute overtime period.

Our last shot attempt missed.

Houston called time-out. I told the team, "Fellas, there is one second left *and more than enough time to lose it* if we aren't concentrating." Rodney McCray, their small forward, sent the ball flying in from out-of-bounds, and I saw all seven feet and four inches of Ralph Sampson go up for it, twisting in the air as the ball touched his hands. Kareem Abdul-Jabbar was hovering between him and the hoop. Sampson literally did not have enough time to let his feet touch the floor again.

While still twisting in midair, he managed to flip a shot in the direction of the basket before the final buzzer could sound.

Later on, Sampson called it "a funky shot." Somehow it caught the rigid heel of the rim. Then it bounced straight up, climbing as high as the top of the backboard. Then it sank through the net like a boulder tumbling into the ocean. Michael Cooper, who had positioned himself in front of the rim for a rebound, dropped flat on his back. As the Houston players began to leap into each other's arms, Coop covered his eyes. The cameras hovered over him for a moment or two, then cut to the exultant new Western Conference champs relishing their moment. That forlorn, blown-down scarecrow image of Michael Cooper captured what we felt. Complacency had come to collect.

Sampson's shot wasn't funky. It was a miracle. It set the stage for learning, growth, and our greatest achievement, which was just around the corner. I love that shot. I love how it was to jolt the smugness out of our hearts.

Anyone who's tasted great success must always ask the next question: what do you do after your dreams have come true? David Stern knows the answer. The Lakers were to learn the answer. How about you?

Time-Out

Breakthroughs crack the hold of the Choke, but they are a heady rush and can also lead to arrogance and a lazy indifference. After the most awesome Breakthroughs, the most crippling team disease of all—Complacency—can begin its sinister growth. If it does, effort, attitude, and diligence are all casualties. Having made it this far along the cycle, Complacency is the last hurdle standing between any team and its potential greatness. Winners vaccinate themselves against self-satisfaction by remembering that some rival is always planning smarter and working harder to overtake and unseat a winner.

8

Mastery

"I'm a great believer in luck, and I find the harder I work, the more I have of it."
—*Thomas Jefferson*

"The will to win is important, but the will to prepare is vital."
—*Joe Paterno*

I n 1961, in the middle of my high school years, a movie came to town that hit my teenage mind like a ton of bricks. It was *The Hustler*, starring Paul Newman as Fast Eddie Felson, an itinerant pool shark chewing his way through the small-timers to take on Minnesota Fats, *the* legendary player of his time.

I could never buy into the lowlife human side of Eddie Felson, but—with a cuestick—he was an artist, and he had an unceasing drive to be the best. Shooting pool was already a love of mine, but that movie pushed me over the top. I bought my own stick and later took it with me to the University of Kentucky.

My Eddie Felson fantasies got squelched when my coach, Adolph Rupp, took me aside one day and said, "Forget about green felt—I want you to concentrate on the game we play on hardwood." When a sequel to *The Hustler* appeared in 1986, I wanted to see what twenty-five years of graduate studies in the School of Hard Knocks had done to my man Eddie. *The Color of Money* portrayed a hardened and deeply scarred veteran with a sixth sense for picking winners from losers. When he came across a promising youngster named Vincent, who reminded him of his own early self, he knew just what the rookie needed to learn.

The young guy, played by Tom Cruise, had just won a very hot game with some flashy, impressive shots. And he started crowing about it. Newman sat him down and tried to teach him that a hustler has to know how to lose in order to be given a chance to win big. He told him he didn't know the difference between excellent pool and pool excellence. And until he learned that difference, he would stay a small-timer. It's no different in my game. Hustling on a basketball court is a lot more honest effort than hustling a pool game, but both require a knowledge of excellence to win. Excellence is about consistent high performance . . . about knowing how much you have to give, and the right time to give it . . . about being both a student *and* a master of human moves.

Around the time Fast Eddie Felson returned to the screen, the 1986–1987 Lakers faced the challenge of learning the difference between excellent basketball—which we had demonstrated hundreds of times—and basketball excellence—which still lay ahead. We had to study the moves—our opponents' and our own.

Excellence is never having learned enough. A few seasons in competitive sports teaches you how success can lull people. Teams who stay on top know different . . . and they live it: **Excellence is the gradual result of always wanting to do better.**

You also gotta set the stage for people to excel. No attitude lecture can take the place of the environment that leaders create for their people. A sound, energized environment allows excellence to happen because a leader has to help talent *want* to do its best. In the words of Wayne Dyer, the highest form of sanity is living in the present moment. It is also the highest form of discipline: a coach must keep everyone on the team in touch with present-moment realities—knowing where they stand, knowing where they're falling short of their potential . . . and knowing it openly and fairly.

At the start of the 1986–1987 season, the coaching staff of the Lakers unveiled a new program for knowing the right moves. It was called Career Best Effort, and I have to thank Assistant Coach Bill "Bert" Bertka, my Administrator of All Things, for helping to design and maintain the system.

Career Best Effort was a system steeped in numbers and measurement, but we weren't just talking about points and statistics. Like any true quest for excellence, it reached for the best in body, mind, and spirit. Unlike most reviews of player performance, which arbitrarily rake people over the coals, this system focuses on the positive use of information. We were out to give the players a clear picture of how they were doing, where they stood, and where to focus their fullest concentration.

Complacency, the thief that stole our previous season's hopes, can exist only in an atmosphere of denial. It just can't survive in an environment of knowing. If relevant facts are assembled and pre-

> "You cannot manage men into battle. You manage things; you lead people."
> —*Grace Murray Hopper*

> "It's what you learn *after* you know it all that counts."
> —*John Wooden*

sented in a clear, openhearted way; reality is defined and denial becomes an impossibility.

The core of the Career Best Effort program was a detailed record-keeping system that the team had been steadily refining over the years.

When players first joined the team, we tracked their basketball statistics all the way back to high school. We called this "taking their number." We used those figures to create an accurate gauge—both of what a player could do and also what that player had to produce in order to lift the team to basketball excellence.

It was a great system, but it needed to be better before the team could get better. We had always ranked a player's performance against that of his teammates until someone pointed out that these comparisons were self-defeating. "It doesn't matter how hard I try," one of them complained, "when I'm compared to Kareem or Earvin, I'm gonna look like dogmeat." He was right. All NBA players are outstanding athletes with highly polished skills, but only a few can rank among the greatest basketball stars of all time. Player input like this later proved crucial to the design and the success of the program.

For the 1986–1987 season we introduced two innovations in our comparisons. Our goal was to leverage subtle improvements versus other high-level competitors. Tremendous is the only word I can use to sum up the impact it delivered.

First, instead of ranking our players against each other, we began comparing them to people on opposing teams with similar positions and similar role definitions. Our starting point guard against everyone else's. Our first reserve power forward against everyone else's. And so on, from the core members down to the last person at the end of the bench. *Everybody had a category in which they could—at least potentially—rank number one in the NBA.*

The second change was to sharpen our historical comparisons. We stacked November of 1986 against November of 1985, for example, to show our players whether they were doing better or worse than at the same point last season. One month later we showed them how their performance in December of 1986 compared to their performance in November of 1986. And we calculated the most productive months of their basketball lives for use as each player's ultimate personal yardstick.

The numbers were used to define a goal that was simple and realistic, yet they could thrust us ahead toward an incredible improvement. From a list of fifteen possible measures, we selected five that had really cost us the last championship. These defined five "trigger points," five areas which comprised the basis of basketball performance for each role and position. We challenged each player to put forth enough effort to gain just one percentage point in each of those five areas. We defined each player's career best effort in each area and said, "Don't try to go 10 percent above it. And don't let yourself go 10 percent below it. Just concentrate on a moderate, sustainable improvement." As we saw it, a one percent improvement in five areas for twelve players gave us a 60 percent increment!

"Those who cannot remember the past are condemned to repeat it."
—*George Santayana*

If this program succeeded, the collective effect would create whole percentage points of improvement, teamwide. Numbers-crunching drove moderate, sustainable team growth: we made stretching beyond present levels of success both a habit and a system.

To work, the system also had to measure effort. Points, rebounds, and assists are the traditional measures of basketball performance. Taken alone, they're a limp yardstick. These old standbys can describe excellent basketball, but they don't define basketball excellence. Effort is the path to excellence. But, how do you put a number on *trying?* They might not be able to describe it, but—believe me—Eddie Felson and any other serious student of human moves would know where to look. You just have to see and count the smaller components that add up to effort.

Riles' Rule of Comparison

Every member on a team plays a different role and brings different skills. For a team made up of highly specialized players, the worst way to compare performance is between each other. The best basis is versus the player's finest counterparts on competing teams or against his own history.

In basketball, these smaller action slices aren't usually data that's recorded. They can nevertheless change the flow of a game. These extraordinary effort plays include stepping in front of the driver and taking the charge full force, so a foul will be called; diving to the floor to take possession of a loose ball; going after rebounds whether you get them or not; stepping up to help a teammate when the player he's guarding has surged past. It adds up to identifying and rewarding "unsung hero" deeds. What, for example, does a player do when the ball is in flight, headed for the basket? A power forward should go after at least forty-five out of fifty possible rebounds. In our system, that would translate to a 90 percent rebound effort. Every important task and action slice like these would be recorded and analyzed.

We developed charts in all areas—defense, rebounding, shot-contesting, and others. One shot chart analyzed a player's accuracy from any point on the floor. We also assessed micro-team performance: what our power forwards, as a playing unit, were doing versus other power forwards in the league; what our point guards did against those we played last night; and so on.

Riles, what are you talking about?! Aren't you just piling on more and more time-and-motion studies? In fact, micro time-and-motion studies driven down to a gnat's eyelash? Don't you know that time-and-motion studies are considered to be degrading and inhuman, and that pricey management consultants preach that kind of stopwatch punching violates the Geneva Convention? Well, I *had* heard that, and I still thought their use was okay for us because basketball is the purest game of time and motion around. Now I feel even better about them.

One morning not long ago, I was leafing through the *Harvard Business Review* and landed on an article by Paul S. Adler, a business school professor at the University of Southern California. The article was titled: "Time-and-Motion Regained." It should be required reading for anybody running any business whose workers constantly repeat certain tasks—from a grocery cashier to a drill press operator. "Formal work standards developed by industrial engineers and imposed on workers *are* alienating," Adler writes. "But procedures that are designed by the workers themselves in a continuous successful effort to improve productivity, quality, skills, and understanding can humanize even the most disciplined forms of bureaucracy." If the assistant coaches, trainers, and I had not shared in the Core Covenant of the team, Career Best Effort would never have worked. If the players hadn't become the most avid users of the system, and actually helped us define and refine the measures, it certainly wouldn't have worked. And, do you know where all this breakthrough evidence on time-and-motion studies was learned? At the NUMMI plant we visited in chapter 1!

The action slices that are the heart of Career Best Effort (or of most people's everyday work) sure don't have the glamour or sizzle of a slam dunk. They don't always look pretty or win applause, and perfecting them takes hard work. But, surely in basketball, making them a habit pays off. Not every time. Maybe not in every game. But sooner or later one of these effort disciplines busts a game wide open. When the opposition's talent and experience levels are bumping up against your own, sustained effort creates a durable edge. Over the course of a season or a fiscal year there is always a match-up between sustained effort and winning.

"He that will not apply new remedies must expect new evils."
—*Francis Bacon*

Cargill, Incorporated—an enormous, privately held Midwestern company—is learning that. It began over one and a quarter centuries ago, trading in agricultural commodities. Over the decades it has diversified into several interrelated divisions that employ some sixty thousand people in more than fifty countries. Look down practically any aisle of any typical grocery store: Cargill is involved, one way or another, in making many of the products you will see.

As a company with a long history of success, Cargill—like the Lakers—had a built-in cushion. Whenever one division had an off-year, another one took up the slack. Facing a period of rapid expansion, Cargill's management realized that they needed to do better and to tighten their efficiency, their cohesiveness, and their team identity.

In September of 1992, Cargill invited me to address their executives. The topic was how to coach people, how to create trusting, empowering relationships within a team. The message I delivered came straight out of the Lakers' Career Best Effort system.

Cargill has now committed to spending $2 million next year on training its employees for sustained high performance, both as individuals and as team players. Their performance appraisal system hits the key skills and traits the Cargill employee of the future will need and links those abilities to the company's business strategy. Not all the skills, I'm sure, can be measured mechanically, but I'll bet they're all measured pretty specifically. As it was for the Lakers, the core effort will be the creation of an accurate picture and then following through until everyone has seen that picture in full.

Facts were the pillar of our system, as it is in any good appraisal program. The numbers were never subjective. They were always rooted in observed and recorded moments of game-time performance. At first, some guys had a hard time accepting the Career Best Effort system. They feared it was the organization's way of cutting their pride, keep-

"Lord, deliver me from the man who never makes a mistake, and also from the man who makes the same mistake twice."
—*Dr. William J. Mayo*

ing them too humble to ask for a raise. But players relate to statistics—if they are coupled with a coach's sincere and competent interpretation—and it didn't take them long to see that the numbers were objective and provided an accurate, fair picture of who was and wasn't giving their best.

We would always post the newest numbers in a plastic sleeve on the front of each player's locker. Before a couple of months had gone by, the players developed a keen interest in these charts. They wanted to know where they stood. Anybody does.

Several of our players, including Kurt Rambis, Byron Scott, and Michael Cooper, were soon performing far above their levels of the previous season. Two of them—A. C. Green and Earvin Johnson—turned 1986–1987 into the best season of their lives. Earvin was eventually named Most Valuable Player in the entire league. Not surprisingly, our system showed that he had the NBA's highest efficiency rating.

Numbers are one part of the performance analysis that leads to mastery. Images are another. We live in a VCR world. High-tech information about performance is crucial. Athletics are a natural for it. I'm an intense editor of video data, and I like to pull together scenes and concepts along themed lines. The players have the chance to look at one player opponent moving against a variety of defenders, or we will review one team's entire range of defensive tactics. When a player gets to see himself doing the same mistake time and again, for example, (or the same right thing, for that matter) it can sharpen a major mental edge.

Anybody whose business requires face-to-face contact with other people lives in a similar world of Showtime. That's the heart of being in a service

"Don't brood on what's past, but don't forget it either."
—Thomas H. Raddal

industry, and I'm surprised that more firms don't do videos of simulated customer service drills. Even meetings: if a work team were forced to look at how they flick issues around a conference table and how they stall putting the decision through the basket, plenty of meetings would be much shorter and more to the point.

Inspiration is another big selling point for gearing up video in a business. The reason: how big can a company team be? Believing that a whole company can be a team is unrealistic. How the hell can fifty-five thousand people interlace? A team can't function together beyond those people its members immediately know or with whom they interact. Otherwise it's a team stitched together with memos, not by a vision of achieving or keeping championship status. "One British furniture company," said another recent *Harvard Business Review* article, "had a rule that it would only grow outward, not upward. No business unit would contain more than 100 people. So as the company prospered, it built new factories and minibusinesses." It understood the importance of keeping the immediate team unit manageable. But the article also goes on to say that the company got into trouble when the economy turned downward. The powers at headquarters were too weak to solve key problems. Divisions ended up competing with each other. The company had built the teams at the right level, but the voice at the center wasn't strong enough to keep those individual teams truly together. You must have *both*.

In big companies, you have to build a lot of little teams which are led by a single voice. The little teams must be drawn together in a common purpose, and video gives you that chance. When I speak to corporations, I almost always have to strike a Covenant with management: "I talk for an hour and fire them up," I'll tell the executives, "but what are you going to do for them next month, or six months from now, when the glow has worn off?" That's why telecommunications and video uplinks make such sense. The satellite is out there spinning through space ready and waiting to do the firing-up. That's how you keep attitude up these days.

Riles' Rule of Micro-Teams

Why do athletic teams inspire people so often? Because they are small enough to be *real teams*. Big companies try to be teams, and so do large government departments, but most can be teams only in very general terms. The micro-team is the core team:

- It must work together almost daily.
- It must be constantly aware of its own performance.
- And it must be in tune with its own morale.

If it can't do these things, the group is not a real team, but a figment of the personnel department's imagination.

Morale is the lifeblood of any team. After running roughshod over the league for years, the Lakers flunked out of the Western Conference Finals in four straight losses in 1986. For the first time in my head coaching career, we had failed to reach the championship round, let alone win it. The Career Best System was a way to address morale. After our Houston debacle in the 1986 playoffs, we were crestfallen. And there was no guarantee that we would immediately start winning games again. But we knew that bringing the effort areas back up would build better morale. Eventually the improvements in effort and in morale would show up as wins. That was our article of faith. It wasn't long before it got put to the test.

Any team that gets trapped into a complacency-caused failure can be sure of one thing: plenty of people will be watching their next step. "How the Mighty Have Fallen" is a surefire plot to draw crowds to a spectacle. NBA schedule-makers knew that when they lined up our first game of the 1986–1987 season on national television versus the Houston Rockets. And we played the spectacle script out perfectly. We showed up, but we *non-competed* ourselves into a 112–102 defeat.

Now we had five consecutive losses to Houston in a five-month span. Lots of people believed the Lakers' era was played out. Showtime basketball was giving way to Twin Tower basketball, and there was a growing gospel that any team *had* to field two seven-footers at once to be a contender. The "experts" were ready to shovel dirt on our coffins. In reality, we were about to stop our downturn. That opening-day loss convinced us how much work was needed, and that our pride commanded us to make the effort. It worked. By Thanksgiving day of 1986 we had put together a string of nine straight victories and were back on top of the Western Conference.

Returning to success after a derailment isn't all a matter of effort and morale. Sometimes you have to augment the team.

The Lakers particularly needed depth at the reserve center position. Kareem's backup from the

"An expert is one who knows more and more about less and less."
—*Nicholas Murray Butler*

171

previous year, Petur Gudmundsson, had gone down with a disc injury in training camp. A week into the season, we had picked up a big, strong, hardworking kid named Mike Smrek, but, growing up in Canada, he had trained in hockey instead of basketball. Anytime Kareem needed a rest, the dropoff in skill level was extreme. We needed a versatile, thoroughly skilled player right now.

On Friday, February 13th, only hours before the trading deadline, Jerry West finished up a deal that brought us Mychal Thompson. The Boston Celtics arrived in our arena just two days later for a nationally televised game. They were the defending champions and, by winning ten of their eleven previous games, they came to town tied with us for the best record in the NBA. Kevin McHale was in peak form. A few nights before, at Denver, he had scored the team's first eleven points.

While we suffered rough spots and turnovers, Boston played flawlessly through the first half and built an eight-point lead. The second half opened with a shooting clinic, taught by Larry Bird and Kevin McHale. By the middle of the third period we were down in the swamp, trailing by seventeen points. Then Mychal Thompson combined with some of the starters to tear off a fourteen-to-two run in five minutes. It's rare for a new player to mesh right away, but Mychal was a rare player. When the game was all over, he had deflected two enemy passes and given a ten-point, four-rebound performance in a 106–103 win. Getting the missing part reclaimed our status as the winningest team in the league.

Of course, augmenting the team is only helpful when you understand exactly what part to add, and how to manage the results. One season before our Career Best Effort plan, we had acquired a veteran power forward named Maurice Lucas to augment our rebounding. Luke did the job. He became the team's number one rebound performer. But the more rebounds he pulled down, the less effort our other guys put into their own rebounding.

Riles' Rule of the Missing Part

Whenever a team augments itself with a "missing part," odds are high others will slack off in areas where this specialist is strong. Only if leadership monitors the impact of the addition and acts as Enforcer, can the "missing part's" boost be upheld throughout the system.

We were in danger of repeating this same syndrome with Mychal Thompson. He made an instant impact. We were winning. But our overall effort level began to slip. It was Mychal's effort that was putting us over the top. That meant we were in danger of repeating last year's problems.

As February of 1992 was coming to a close, we had a seven-game win streak going. We played Utah on the 28th, on the road. After that we would be able to relax a little because we were playing eight of the next nine games at home.

Trouble simmered as soon as we got off the plane at Salt Lake City. It was only ten in the morning, but the players dragged through baggage claim and onto the team bus like it was the end of a double-shift day at the factory. On the bus, I asked the trainer to spread the word that we would change at the hotel and go straight across the street for a brief practice and preparation. Nothing extensive, just a walk-through and some free-throw shooting, then the rest of the day open until evening game time. The whole bus went stonily silent. The practice was sullen. Their body language said, "I'll do what I'm told—but beyond that I expect to be left alone!"

Four minutes into the game, we were already down by eleven to three. Mychal Thompson and a couple of other reserves played hard, but, overall, we wouldn't compete. There was a flash of effort in the fourth quarter, enough to bring us within three points, followed by a near-total letdown. We came out on the wrong side of a 107–100 final score.

As we filed into the locker room, I circled in as everyone got settled, letting the mood of the loss sink in for a minute or two. Then I verbally ripped into the team with a passion I hadn't shown them since the Memorial Day Massacre. My comments were brutally frank—not about any one person, but rather about the team as a whole: their lack of fire, their declining effort levels, their mistaken notion that a closing-minutes effort could cancel out all the negatives. I repeatedly used the word "quit," the word players hate most of all.

"We quit when it got tough, just like last year's playoffs."

No player wants to be known as a quitter. We had the best record in the league, we had lost only one game in eight, and I was calling them the lowest thing you can call an athlete. They had to be shaken, brought back to the reality of what we were trying to accomplish. "You don't owe me anything," I said, "you owe each other. You quit on each other, out on the court, and that cost you the game."

I was railing against the same factors that had

"Some of us are like wheelbarrows—only useful when pushed, and very easily upset."
—*Jack Herbert*

demolished us one year ago. You see, no matter how much progress a team or an individual makes, no matter how much they lift their aspirations and their performance, old behavior patterns will always try to prevail. You simply have to be wise to yourself. Know your own style of backsliding, catch it as early as possible and turn it around.

My talk was done, but the outburst needed a punctuation mark. A couple of huge plastic bags were slumped on the floor. They were half filled with ice and straight on my path to the door. As I stormed out, I nailed them both with a sideways, soccer-style kick that burst the plastic and sent cubes and water spraying in every direction.

When I yanked the locker room door open, the team saw an "I Love Lucy" sketch come to life: a beat reporter was crouched down low, with his right ear positioned for eavesdropping. The backdraft of the swinging door almost sucked him into the room on all fours.

The Temporary Insanity Textbook

- A leader's aggrieved outburst is not an explosion, nor is it a regular or predictable event.
- It is the art of being angry at the right time, to the right degree, with the right people.
- T.I. requires plenty of advanced thought—a real and focused mental plan, not emotion-driven monologue.
- A dose of T.I. demands a rapid follow-up of compassion.
- The T.I. leader should always send out someone to complete the damage report and to get a quick, accurate reading of the emotional wounding done by the rampage.

Compassion is vital. Without it, anger degenerates into brutality and tears the fabric of the team. As much as possible, a positive emotional environment has to govern the team. After my tirade there was a lingering sense of estrangement. At the start of our first practice after the Utah loss, the players remained very quiet in my presence. When the stretching exercises were over, Earvin looked up at me and said, "Uh, Riles, could the team have a meeting by ourselves?"

"Sure," I said.

I don't know what message he gave them, but that turned into one of our best workouts in weeks. Over the next five games our overall efficiency rating rose by two hundred points. Afterward I had a private talk with Earvin about what had happened in the Utah locker room.

"What did you think?" I asked. "Was it good or bad?"

"It was good and it was bad," he said. "It was good because you really got us thinking. It was bad because you scared the hell out of half the guys. Some of them don't know you like I know you. Some of them had their jaws hit the floor. They were wondering 'Why me? How come he's blaming me?' "

The fact is every moment of that Temporary Insanity was pre-thought in word and gesture. I never once pointed out any one individual. But the guys who knew they were guilty of withholding effort thought I was talking straight to them.

We went on to win ten in a row, and clinched the Pacific Division title when we beat the Pistons on March 26th. Two days later came a very satisfying win over our tour nemesis of the previous spring, the Houston Rockets.

We finished with a record of sixty-five wins and seventeen losses, our best single-season record of the 1980s. Just before half time in game one of our first playoff series, a three-game sweep of Denver, Earvin threw in a length-of-court shot at the buzzer that gave us a playoff scoring record: eighty-two points in a half.

In the second round, we were going for a sweep in game four against Golden State when Sleepy Floyd delivered one of the most remarkable shooting performances in playoff history: twenty-two points in the first three quarters, followed by an incredible twenty-nine in the final twelve minutes.

Floyd's hot shooting had built a lead for Golden State, but we overcame it to go ahead. It looked like we were going to close them out. Some of our players began to chest-bump each other, gesturing, taunting, defusing their own energies, but they also got the opponents' juices boiling, too. Our egotistical, puffed-up pride jarred us out of focus and inspired Golden State to win.

After that loss we held a team meeting. I showed them a series of fresh headlines out of Dallas. The Dallas Mavericks were the Midwest Division's top team that year, fourth-best in the entire league. Their opening round matchup had been the Supersonics, a team that had barely squeaked into the playoffs. Dallas had won the first game going away, 151–129. The hometown headline said, DALLAS RIPS SONICS, LOOKS FOR SWEEP. But Seattle had eked out a two-point win in game two. The next headline said, DALLAS GETS NIPPED, SERIES TIED. Now the action had shifted to Seattle's home court. So had the momentum. Game three came down to SEATTLE DESTROYS MAVERICKS.

Two days later came a twenty-six-point Seattle win and a headline that read, DALLAS CHOKES.

All of this within six short days.

I said, "You just gave Golden State an edge. The question is, do you want to read the same kind of headlines in the *Los Angeles Times*? After what we went through last year?"

We got our heads back on straight, completed the series in game five, then swept Seattle out of the conference finals, coming back from twenty-nine down in the second period of game four.

Because the Eastern Conference championship was still up for grabs between Boston and Detroit, we suddenly had about nine days' time on our hands. I walked into the locker room on the morning of a light practice. When I looked at Earvin Johnson, he was already looking at me, as if he was wondering whether I was thinking what he was thinking. "Coach," he said, "we've got to get out of town. We don't want to stay in Los Angeles the whole time. Where do we want to go?"

When you get to the point of competing for the pinnacle of your profession, you don't want to hold anything back. Knowing you might not get the opportunity again, knowing that you've dodged all the land mines, you still must deal with fear. We decided to take the team to Santa Barbara, away from home front distractions, to stage a miniature version of training camp. The idea was to renew our commitment to the Career Best System, to recharge our devotion to efficiency and effort instead of relying on our talent to carry the day.

We came out of Santa Barbara as an electro-charged team, running and passing and shooting with totally focused energy, complete precision. We were ready to play for a championship.

The 1987 NBA Finals began early in the evening of June 2nd, as Jake O'Donnell lofted the ball at center court between Kareem Abdul-Jabbar and Robert Parish of the Boston Celtics. It was, like any Boston/L.A. matchup of the 1980s, a series full of extraordinary moments and incredible courage on both sides. Hard-fought every inch of the way. But we had something fantastic on tap—basketball excellence—the result of focusing all season long on the realities of the present moment, and applying all our concentration to the job of continually becoming better.

One play dominates my memory. It was early in the third quarter of game six, on our home court, when we were trailing by one point. We had been behind almost the entire game.

We had played terrifically in the first two games, and we had won them both. Boston then pulled out a six-point victory in game three, lost by only one point in game four, and kicked us from pillar to post, 123–108, in game five.

Game six brought us back to our home court. We were in a position either to win it all or drop into a three-three tie, as I loaded my attaché case with another change of clothes.

The pressure made us play ahead of the moment—a little too tight, a little afraid to trust our instincts. Pushing, rushing, instead of letting our game flow. We were down five points at half time. We were gaining on them slowly in the early third quarter, but still overtightened, tentative.

The key difference between ordinary and extraordinary players is that the great ones are always thinking one, two, or three plays ahead. James Worthy had been laying sort of half-hidden in the weeds when Kevin McHale attempted a pass out of the post to Dennis Johnson during the third quarter. James, shooting the gap, made the steal of the year. His fingertips deflected the ball at an angle crossing the Lakers' end of the court, but projected toward the sideline. Rather than let the ball go out-of-bounds, he sprinted in its direction.

Earvin, also thinking ahead of the play, saw what might unfold. While James sprinted after the ball, he began a loping stride down the middle of the court. James, operating at the outer limits of his exceptional body control, launched himself facefirst at the ball just before it could go out. In midflight, he caught a glimpse of Earvin's position. Just before completing a half-turn in the air and skidding on his back across the hardwood for two or three body lengths, he stretched his left arm to full extension and managed to flick the ball toward his teammate. At the end of his horizontal slide, James was able to lift his head for a good look at Earvin jamming the ball through the hoop, giving us the lead.

"We take eagles and teach them to fly in formation."
—D. Wayne Calloway

It was a single play, created by the habit of sustained effort, that busted open the game and won the championship. It was the mirror opposite of last year's lethargy. Earvin's bucket became the first of an eighteen-to-two run that put us out in front by thirteen points.

In the fourth quarter, Kareem gave one of the most legendary performances of his career—scoring fourteen of his game-high thirty-two points while drawing fouls number five on McHale and number six on Parish. When they won, 106–93, the Lakers served notice that we were more than just an excellent team. We embodied team excellence.

The joy in the locker room—champagne spraying into every corner, wives, friends, and broadcasters all sharing the moment—lasted for a good two hours, yet it felt like barely fifteen minutes. But the afterglow has never gone away.

That's how you feel when something significant has been achieved.

Did my outrage in the Utah locker room get us to the victory parade? Or was it the result of a system that identified and rewarded Career Best Effort, put into practice among a group of proud athletes who, collectively, had been evolving their winning ways for a long time? What was the force that led us to mastery? Did it all begin with what Ralph Sampson called his "funky" shot?

Fast Eddie Felson would know the answer. So do the folks at the NUMMI plant in California. So would the championship-team Lakers. They all got there through an unceasing drive to be the best. They would also all tell you that hard, intelligent, relentless work is the way to winning. Excellence is the way. Mastery is the way. Challenge is the way.

"If you can dream it, you can do it. Always remember that this whole thing was started by a mouse."
—*Walt Disney*

Time-Out

Only by committing oneself to a tougher and constant standard of training, alertness, and performance can Complacency be kept at bay. Mastery is the next goal, and Mastery is built on excellence— the gradual result of always wanting to do better. Mastery demands an intense awareness of the present moment and keen knowledge of one's individual best-effort potential. In getting to Mastery, no matter what the team or contest, precise and clearly understood information is the foundation. Mastery is as emotional as it is mental. You can't attain Mastery and neglect morale . . . and morale isn't simply encouragement. It is sparked by the will of a team's coach and its leadership to challenge the team defiantly to reach for tougher new standards.

9
Upping the Ante

"I would sooner fail than not be among the greatest."
—*John Keats*

"To be what we are, and to become what we are capable of becoming, is the only end of life."
—*Robert Louis Stevenson*

M
y father-in-law, Frank Rodstrom, is seventy-seven. We share the same birthday, and I like to think that we have more in common, too.

Frank is 5'11", athletic, and has a great coaching "voice." It's patient, steady, but by no means soft or undemanding—and it's easy to understand where Chris got some of her own determination and sense of mission.

In fact, there's no one I know personally who has experienced the meaning of being on a mission in a more vivid, life-or-death way than Frank. In 1934 Frank joined the Navy as an apprentice seaman. After training, he shipped out on his first submarine—the USS *S-21*, an old World War I type. He spent most of the next decade with the submarine force homeported at Pearl Harbor. Frank's mission—and that of his crewmates—was literally to sink Japan dead in the water, ideally without getting killed in the process.

Submarine warfare is teamwork at its peak. It's your life—not a profit-or-loss or a game win—that hinges on the performance of other people. When you dive, all the hull openings better be closed. In World War II, that demanded the reaction time and the vigilance of people, not computers. If a Zero fighter were whizzing in, and you didn't clear the bridge fast enough, you would put the mission, the ship, and the lives of the entire crew in immediate jeopardy. Just like pro basketball, a great many more people fantasized about being submariners than were really cut out to play the game. The sub school graduated only five hundred of the fifteen hundred it would take on for training.

World War II submarine crews were very young. The skippers were thirty-two or so. The crew averaged twenty-one to twenty-five, and every one of them was a volunteer. American submarine-personnel policies created an excellent experience mix. After returning from patrol, a skipper had to surrender 25 percent of his team to the replacement pool and to start-up crews for newly built submarines. The fillback was mostly recent sub-school graduates. There was an above-average intelligence requirement for sub duty, and that—plus extra pay—added a positive sense of elitism. The sub school was also very strict, weeding out people who weren't suited for that kind of duty, especially ones with the wrong psychological makeup.

"It's a strange kind of tension," Frank recalls, "being off a beautiful tropical island with the sun glistening on the ocean, knowing that there are people hunting for you in subs and antisub ships who are out to kill you while you're out to kill them. Nothing did a better job of reminding us that this was not paradise and of keeping us sharp than periodically spotting an enemy periscope.

"I'll never forget my first patrol on the USS *Pogy*. It was off the Japanese coast. I was a chief petty officer and an underwater sound operator. Enemy shipping was our target, and we had already taken out one ship ferrying high explosives. The explosion was colossal. We may have accomplished our mission, but we were also now hunted game for every Japanese patrol around us. For the next few days, we sweated as we prowled for more kills. Then we spotted an unescorted two-ship convoy and scored a hit, but the skipper kept the periscope up a bit too long in firing on both ships. Suddenly we had incoming aircraft on us, and a bomb exploded over our stern. It felt like we had been whalloped by a huge sledgehammer. It slammed the sub's nose into the air. Mercury splashed out of the gyro compasses, so we could no longer tell where we were. And, to boot, we still had two torpedoes running hot in the tubes."

After that attack, Frank says, they went deep and tried to evade. The customary, eerie quiet set in. "When you knew depth charges might be in the cards, all the ventilating equipment would be turned off. And we waited for what seemed like hours for the first depth charge to go off. We had all stripped down to our typical undersea battle uniform of shorts and submarine sandals. It was so hot you could wring out a leather belt. *Nothing brings a team closer together than being depth-charged.*"

Then it came. As sound operator, Frank got the

"The object of war is not to die for your country, but to make the other bastard die for his."
—*General George Patton*

news first that the sub was under attack: "When a charge is released, you hear a click, and then a swish as the current of displaced water swims through the sub's superstructure. The interval between the click and the swish tells you about how far away the guy is. Short interval and I'd be the first to know that the next swish on the agenda would be the Grim Reaper's. That one missed, but not by much. There were a few more swishes, but each fainter than the last. Over the deathly silence of the sub, you could then hear the breathing of the crewmates, louder than the swishes. After what seemed like ages, Skip turned on the ventilators. We all exhaled, almost like a chorus. We had achieved the mission . . . and we had survived our achievement."

After harrowing times, the skipper might put out a little bottle of brandy, and he did this time, Frank says. But what was it that really held this team together? According to Frank it was the *mission beyond:* the constant training for the time that they weren't on watch, asleep or at battle stations. Once underway on a mission, everybody went to school, each officer or junior officer took a group of men and held a school for their peers. After becoming an officer, Frank specialized in administration. The other two on board who had come up through the ranks were a navigator and a machinist. They would train each other in four-hour stints. The captain said if the war lasted long enough, we would be skippers and he wanted to make sure we were trained. "It gave us a longer-term sense of Mission that went beyond the immediate mission we were on," Frank believes, "and obviously it made the team more competent and interchangeable, too."

"A mission could be defined as an image of a desired state that you want to get to. Once fully seen, it will inspire you to act, fuel your motivation and determine your behavior."
—*Charles Garfield*

By the end of the war, the underwater offensive against Japan had been so successful that two hundred U.S. submarines were closing in on the Land of the Rising Sun. They said that you could walk to Tokyo on periscopes. Winners like Frank Rodstrom were certainly one of the reasons why. After the war, Frank became an EDP ace and was instrumental in setting up a mechanized personnel accounting and distribution system that better utilized naval personnel. Later he was a distinguished executive in private life. In everything he's done, Frank's known his Mission and achieved it.

Riles' Rule for Footprints

Having a sense of Mission that reaches beyond the present defines the final steps to individual and team significance. That means going beyond simply being the best, going so far that you leave footprints.

In your whole life, in your whole career, there may be only two or three times when you're truly on a Mission of greatness. When you are, you have to know how to behave, how to perceive, and how to carry through.

The Los Angeles Lakers began a Mission on June 14th, 1987, in the first minutes of a long, crazed, joyous locker room celebration after beating the Celtics. We had just ended a great comeback year with a championship. Champagne was dripping off my hair, my shoulders, rolling down me until it soaked my shoes and socks. The level of emotion in the room was escalating second by second. A mass of reporters gathered in front of me and thrust microphones into my face: "What about it, coach?" one guy asked in a testing tone. "Can you win again next year?"

At a moment like this, there's a certain way you're expected to act. You're supposed to do a Jimmy Stewart–style "Aw, shucks," clasp your hands behind your back, bow your head and say: "Maybe. I sure hope so. If we can stay healthy, if luck stays with us, then, gosh, we might have a chance."

"Fortune favors the bold."
—*Virgil*

I knocked all that crap aside. I flat-out *guaranteed* all those reporters that we would do it again.

One of my players overheard the exchange. As soon as the reporters drifted to another corner of the celebration, he looked at me and said, "Riles, you ought to keep that champagne on the *outside* of your head!" He was dead serious. In this moment of high spirits, I was putting a weight on his shoulders, already beginning to coach for the next year.

But I wasn't drunk, not with champagne nor glory nor bravado. A sober calculation signed that guarantee. A good coach never stops coaching, and I knew that it was time for this team to embark on a Mission.

"Impossible is a word to be found only in the dictionary of fools."
—*Napoleon Bonaparte*

I repeated that guarantee the next day to the thousands upon thousands of people at our victory parade, and the effect was electric. Every TV station in Los Angeles broadcast the message that evening. There was no backing down.

As the 1987 playoffs wound down, I thought a great deal about that moment. The more thought I gave it, the more I realized that all the ifs, ands, and buts—all the qualifications—traditionally uttered by coaches and leaders after great moments, were nothing but failure messages in disguise. They were a subconscious way of taking off the pressure, making sure that the back door was opened so teams could escape the demands of their own greatness.

The Lakers didn't need to head into the coming season padded with pre-planned excuses. I wanted them to feel the pressure right away, and to spend their off-season deciding that they would shoulder every bit of it.

Riles' Rule for Raising the Stakes

Coaches who let a championship team back off from becoming a dynasty are cowards. But if you raise the ante, make sure you are flush with resources and drive. You'll have to be prepared to wager the team's total wherewithal—and yours too—to win dynasty stakes.

At the start of a Mission, two traits have to come on-line. One is courage and the other is resolve. I like Mark Twain's definition of courage: "Courage is resistance to fear, mastery of fear—not absence of fear." Frank Rodstrom has told me that being "scared to death" was a condition of life in submarine warfare in the South Pacific. Being afraid is OK, if you are afraid with dignity. To a greater or lesser extent, fear is part of any challenge. That's why that player resented hearing the guarantee in his moment of joy. It reminded him of his fear. Later, we talked it over. He said, "Riles, you shouldn't put that kind of pressure on us. You're not the one who has to go out there and play."

"No," I said, "I don't have to go out there and fight our opponents on the court. But I'm still just as much a part of this team as you are. And I'll suffer the consequences of losing just as much as you will. Somewhere along the way we have to stop being afraid of the consequences. Because when you go for something significant—like we are—consequences become irrelevant. Nothing matters except that we are all in this together."

Through nineteen prior years, every NBA champion had been a one-hit wonder. None had withstood the pressure of winning back-to-back championships. And there were a number of reasons why it was a hell of a challenge.

The Lakers, like any champion, no longer had the motivation of being underdogs. We had to define a new motivation and to spike it with an even greater intensity. We had to be intent on proving, for all time, that we ranked among the greatest teams in basketball history.

Charles Garfield's *Peak Performance* says a Mission is ". . . an image of a desired state that you want to get to. . . . If that image is defined and visualized by everybody, if it is believed in, then the image will determine behavior, it will fuel your motivation and it will inspire you to act."

The Lakers were at such a moment in history. The cycle of the team was winding down. Earvin Johnson, Byron Scott, Michael Cooper, and James Worthy were no longer young. Kareem, after an incredibly long run as King of the Mountain, after setting records for scoring and endurance that will probably never be approached, was close to retirement. We had to feel a sense of urgency. If we were ever going to be the first team to win back-to-back championships, now was the time. We had wasted other, earlier opportunities through choking, complacency, dissension, and our inability to recover from Thunderbolts. History wouldn't allow us the luxury of another comeback.

The guarantee was simply a way of upping the ante. It announced a brand-new theme to the world: "The criterion for basketball greatness is winning back-to-back championships, and that is exactly what this team will do."

The prevailing belief was that nobody could sustain two championship drives. Not in the 1980s. Between the salary cap, draft restrictions designed to enforce parity, and the across-the-board increased skill levels of all players entering the NBA, it had become impossible for any one team to stay dominant. The players made bigger money. Million-dollar-a-year men were becoming commonplace, and so were towering egos. Players often would not hunker down to the team's needs. Injuries were inevitable, and so was team dissension. All great excuses. Why try? Just sit back and play a comfortable losing season as outgoing champs.

But when somebody tells you that you *can't* do the very thing you feel you *must* do, if you're any kind of a competitor, if your makeup has even a trace of *The Winner Within,* you have all the challenge you need. You will go on a Mission.

Companies embark on Missions just as individuals and teams do. I can think of three striking examples from the business world when tremendous success has been the direct outgrowth of a clear Mission: the New York Knicks franchise, HBO, and the Rodale Press.

I said earlier that the NBA has been a marketing bonanza, and one reason is that the owners and management have hitched the NBA to a Mission that is much bigger than shaking a money tree. Marketing is what it's all about in the NBA. But the marketing has some surprising roots. For the most successful franchises, marketing is not about slick

> "The uncommitted life isn't worth living."
> —*Marshall Fishwick*

> "Great ideas need landing gear as well as wings."
> —*C. O. Jackson*

ad campaigns or media hype. Instead, the marketing Mission is rooted in the team's broader purpose.

When we were chatting recently at the Garden, Knicks president Dave Checketts articulated the Mission as clear as crystal: "The fans (who are our consumers in this industry) must take an interest in the franchise. When they talk about the team, they should feel like saying: 'We won' or 'We lost' or 'Did you see our game?' versus 'Those bums lost again.' It's the principle of *community ownership.*" When a community owns its team, Dave believes, they will say, "What are we going to do about the point-guard position?" or "How are we going to draft this year?"

"The emphasis is on *we,*" is how Dave puts it. "They view that admission ticket as their part of the dream—a share of stock." How do you put the community ownership principle to work in a town like New York? "Partly because ad costs in New York are prohibitively expensive, we've adopted almost exclusively a community-relations marketing strategy," says Checketts. "Even putting costs aside, it is the strategy that makes the most sense. The marketing campaign that we have launched over the past two years had to change how people *felt* about us, not how they *thought* about us."

Kids are obviously a core focus of the Mission. "New Yorkers had to see how we were getting kids off of the street to play in the Junior Knicks," says Dave. "We have focused on keeping ninth-grade dropouts in school and putting out antidrug and anti-child-abuse messages. We raise money for wheelchair charities and juvenile diabetes." How does this all fit together? "Because the media are so powerful here, they pick all of that up and it *becomes* the marketing strategy. Every New York is saying 'Why doesn't someone help?' and here's the Knicks—an organized source trying to do some good."

But there's a commercial payoff, too. Community ownership makes people want to wear the name of their team: "It gives me a sense of strength and pride," is their attitude. While the Chicago Bulls are the leading merchandising team in the NBA right now, the Knicks hope to take that slot over at some point. Ticket sales have been booming. And long-range franchise strategy is another factor: "Community ownership also gives a team a certain cushion against times when the team is off or when it is rebuilding," says Dave. "If the fans have a genuine investment in and commitment to the team, they are more inclined to ride out the dry spells."

Riles' Rule of the Cushion

A prudent team creates cushions as insurance against adversity. Average teams lean on those cushions. Outstanding ones use them as springboards to attain the next level of greatness.

Another Mission-driven business that is a master of converting cushions into springboards is the media entertainment company Home Box Office. Back in 1976, the management of HBO took a chance on a thirty-year-old guy named Michael Fuchs. I was introduced to him through a close personal friend years ago. It turned out that we had mutual roots and friends in Schenectady, where I went to high school and he went to college.

When HBO hired Fuchs, they got someone who

absolutely lived and breathed the idea of a Mission. And that was exactly what they needed. The company had been in operation for four years, and there was talk that they might shut down soon. One day Fuchs described the HBO mind-set of the late 1970s to me: "We never took it for granted that we belonged, or that we would always belong. HBO had to hustle."

They were aware that other cable channels would always be competing for their subscribers. Being a conduit for Hollywood films and occasional sports events wasn't enough. They decided to set the pace in original, made-for-cable productions. This is what differentiated their Mission. And they won that game. HBO broadcast the industry's first made-for-cable movie in 1981. A year later they formed a partnership called Tri-Star Pictures with CBS and Columbia Pictures. By 1987 they received the cable industry's first Academy Award. And tremendous growth came along the way, too.

"A wise man will make more opportunities than he finds."
—*Francis Bacon*

Even when the company doubled its revenue projections in a year, Fuchs was smart enough to worry. "That kind of success creates an atmosphere that makes it difficult to be disciplined," he told me. "We were on a continuous fast break. But the rules of the game were going to change. The business would mature. Subscription increases would gradually get harder and harder to achieve. Holding on to those new customers would be more and more vital. We would have to play a half-court game, grinding out each point. We couldn't afford turnovers."

Almost overnight the cable industry lost the wildcat, anything-goes aura of the early and mid-1980s. As it did, Fuchs was ready to spruce up the Mission for running the business, and it worked.

HBO is today the benchmark of the industry, a $1.5 billion business that generates over $200 million in annual profits.

Another company—a publishing firm—that invited me to speak last summer has had the good fortune to be steadily cruising along on a Mission since before the NBA or HBO even existed. All thanks to the publisher's founder.

In the late 1930s, J. I. Rodale was the owner of a prosperous company, a manufacturer of electrical devices. But his heart wasn't in it. He became fascinated by books that taught the good care of soil so it would produce the healthiest possible crops for the longest possible time. As his interest grew, so did his conviction that this was a way to help people making the most of their lives—by living more healthily.

Nowadays, physical fitness is something nearly everyone believes in. When J. I. Rodale got started, an interest in fitness prompted people to write you off as a health nut.

In the early 1940s, he bought a farm in rural Pennsylvania and put his organic gardening ideas to the test. The farm had hardpan, run-down soil, but it gradually turned into some of the most productive land in the region. In May of 1942, Rodale printed the first issue of a magazine called *Organic Farming and Gardening.* By 1950 he was ready to add *Prevention,* a magazine dedicated to personal health.

As the environmental movement took off in the early 1970s, so did Rodale Press. J. I.'s son, Robert, took over and led a gradual expansion, all of it rooted to the original idea of the founder—sharing information that leads to healthier living. Today, Rodale Press is a privately held, family-owned,

$400-million-a-year company. All of their mature magazines are the dominant ones in their field, and they have a book division that has grown rapidly in recent years. While most magazine publishers have suffered shrinking revenues in the last couple of years, Rodale is one of the few that keeps growing in prosperity. Their dedication to a clear Mission, with the cornerstone of health, has made Rodale Press the dynasty in its segment of the publishing industry.

What do these three Missions have in common?

The Winning Mission Recipe

A business Mission is likely to succeed

- if it puts a clear concept above raking in money;
- if the people who must achieve the Mission share in understanding it and are committed to it;
- if the Mission is vigilantly adjusted for changes in competition;
- if the Mission is updated to keep pace with a company's own success;
- if the Mission sets out what's needed to be the best, not just an acceptable, performer in the industry.

Dynasties demand determination. In sports that means you have to return to the workaday world of a new season after waging and winning war on the championship battlefield. It can be hard to muster the intensity you need. When we came back to regular season play after winning a championship, Laker owner Jerry Buss compared it to hopping from a high-stakes poker game to playing at a table with a dollar limit.

> ## Riles' Rule of Reengagement
> After a glorious victory in a grand war, the hardest
> battle to fight is the first little skirmish of the next
> campaign.

Still, the Lakers opened the 1987–1988 season
with eight wins in a row, the best start in club
history. After that we suffered a letdown and lost
six out of nine. Each of those losses was by a
narrow margin, but still they rattled us. We began
to fear how stupid, how vain, how ridiculous we
would look if our back-to-back drive fell flat. Then
Earvin inspired us all with a miracle shot at the
buzzer, an extremely flat-angled bank off the glass,
under pressure, to beat the Boston Celtics on their
home floor. That shot was the starter's pistol for a
fifteen-game win streak.

Gradually, we got in touch with a common
awareness and ambition, and felt the fear and self-
doubt our boldness had triggered drain away. We
arrived at the All-Star break with thirty-five wins
and eight losses.

Then we began to ram into walls. A really tough
stretch of schedule put us up against the Celtics
and the Clippers at home, followed by road games
on consecutive nights with the Rockets and the
Hawks, then one day's rest before going up against
the Pistons in their arena. We won all five, but
along the way Michael Cooper severely sprained an
ankle. It dogged him the rest of the season. On
March 10th, driving the lane against the Bulls in
Chicago, Earvin strained an already-sore groin
muscle and pulled up in extreme pain. Now both
our point guards were in rough shape. Meanwhile,

James Worthy had been struggling for months against patellar tendinitis, sore knees. Kareem's production was declining. A. C. Green had a severe hip bruise. Because we had been contenders year after year, we had actually played more games than any other team in the league. Over time, that additional physical wear and tear had caught up with us.

We had at least a half-dozen perfect excuses to step back from our Mission. But the image of what we wanted was too strong. We held on and finished the year with a record of sixty-two and twenty, best in the NBA.

Then we rolled into playoff competition—not knowing it would turn into the most grueling, punishing postseason run in team history. Several times during the 1988 playoffs, I could have used a booster shot of "faith" concentrate. On June 21st, 1988, one year and one week after the guarantee that we would repeat as champions, I finally understood just how rough a ride it all had been. And it wasn't over yet.

"It is a rough road that leads to the heights of greatness."
—*Seneca*

This realization hit me as I was trying to coach the team through the last couple of minutes of game seven against the Detroit Pistons. This was our twenty-fourth playoff game. After sweeping San Antonio in the opening round, we had run into three brutally hungry teams. Each one of those teams extended us through a full seven-game series. And each one was meaner and more competitive than the one that came before.

The Utah Jazz took us right up to the brink. John Stockton, their magnificent little point guard, carved out records for the most steals and the most assists in a playoff series. Karl Malone scored over two hundred points in the series.

With Mark Eaton blocking seven shots in the first half, the Jazz stole game two on our home court, then dropped us in a deep hole by winning game three. That night we held a meeting in my hotel room, reviewing tapes of both losses. You could see how altitude was playing a part. It's always harder to win at Utah because it's so high in the Rockies and the air is much thinner. For some reason our two biggest stars—Earvin and Kareem—were the guys who were most affected by the altitude. And we were facing a pivotal game. I didn't know what to do except verbally lean on both of them, trying to inspire them to play harder.

"I may not be the lion, but it was left to me to give the lion's roar."
—*Winston Churchill*

Earvin had a tough start in game four. He seemed wounded by what had been said at the meeting and he looked uninspired, as if he thought I didn't believe in him anymore. He wasn't making eye contact with me. We were nine points down in the third quarter when some of the other guys stepped up. For once in his career, Earvin was led by his teammates, feeling their positive peer pressure. It paid off. By the middle of the fourth quarter he was back to his old self, and we won.

Game five put us back on the brink. We were trailing in the closing moment, setting up a play on the sidelines. The Jazz focused their defense on Earvin and Kareem, our moneymen. Michael Cooper inbounded the ball to Earvin, who began penetrating inside, drawing all the defenders with him. Cooper was known for being a defensive specialist. No one paid attention to him as he stepped up to a position behind the three-point line, but Earvin knew he was there and kicked the ball back out, into Coop's hands. The whole championship drive was riding on this shot, and he nailed it. We held on to win. The series was three to two, our favor.

The Jazz answered in game six by handing us the worst defeat in Laker playoff history, a 108–80 loss.

We came back home and scrapped our way to an eleven-point win in game seven. With that, the series closed out and we took a long sigh of relief. I told the press that we had just gotten past the toughest hurdle of the playoffs. I was wrong. Our next opponents, the Dallas Mavericks, had seen us on the ropes, fighting for our lives. That gave them a potent sense of possibility. My statement only added to their fire.

Our first two games against Dallas were both double-digit wins. But then Roy Tarpley came storming off the bench in game three, scoring twenty-one points, grabbing twenty rebounds, keeping them in the game. It came down to a fluke play: we were ahead by two with fifteen seconds left. James Worthy, in making a great effort, went after a loose ball that was about to go out of bounds. He flipped it back onto the court, but it wound up in the hands of their best three-point shooter. We lost by one point. Tarpley sustained his intensity through game four and the Mavericks beat us again. Earvin covered Tarpley in game five and we had a strong win, then we lost game six in the closing seconds. Once again, an underdog team had us backed into a winner-take-all showdown.

Over in the east, our traditional finals adversaries, the Boston Celtics, were also reeling. After struggling through a seven-game series to get by the Hawks, they fell in the Eastern Conference Finals to the very hungry and hard-hitting Detroit

Pistons. An era had ended. As they walked off the floor together, Kevin McHale of the Celtics put an arm around Isiah Thomas of the Pistons and urged him on: "Don't let down. Keep your intensity up until you win the Finals, too."

The practice we held before game seven against Dallas was about the quietest, most focused one I've ever seen. Boston's loss had made a deep impression about our own mortality. That night, Cooper hit two for two from three-point range, while James Worthy scored twenty-eight points and Earvin came within one rebound of a triple-double. We advanced. Once again, it was to meet a team that was more rested than we were.

Detroit had the most dangerous three-guard rotation in the NBA—guys who could get blistering hot streaks going, guys who could out-quick you and slash through your interior defense for layups. In Dennis Rodman they had a rebounding fiend. In Bill Laimbeer they had a brutal enforcer who could also hit the three-point bomb. They put it all together and stunned us by stealing game one at the Forum, 105–93.

That was on a Tuesday. On Wednesday, Earvin came down with the flu. Thursday, in game two, he delivered a forty-two-minute performance that kept us alive.

Then it was our turn to shock the Pistons, beating them 99–86 on their home floor. By way of reply, they whipped us twice in a row—by twenty-five points in game four, then by ten in game five.

For the second time in the playoffs, a challenger had us set up for a knockout punch. All the Pistons had to do was win one out of the next two games and we would be extinct.

They almost got the job done. In spite of a

sprained ankle, Isiah Thomas put on a spectacular show in game six—forty-three points for the game, twenty-five of them in the third quarter. We had a lead in the fourth quarter, then lost it when Detroit staged a nine-to-two run. It all came down to a pair of free throws made by Kareem in the finest Choke-free style you could imagine, giving us a one-point margin. Later I asked Kareem what he had been thinking about when he made those shots. He said: "I liked to get paid." We held on to it, just barely, in the closing seconds. For the third time, our yearlong Mission was down to a winner-take-all gamble.

When the Lakers drew together before the start of game seven, I told them that Detroit was after something big—a championship—but we were after something bigger: a place in history.

Several times in game seven, though, it felt as though we would go belly-up at the moment of truth. We could have put the game out of reach time after time, but we kept letting each chance slip away. We repeatedly made potentially fatal errors, handing opportunities to some of the hungriest, most aggressive opponents ever to play the game.

With each turnover and each off-the-wall shot selection, my fear of losing became stronger. Nevertheless, we were holding on to another one-point lead, 106–105, as the clock wound down to its last seven seconds.

The Pistons were at their most dangerous when they were on defense. Earvin Johnson was dribbling the ball for us during those last seconds, deep in Detroit's court. If he were to get stripped, or to throw the ball away, it would mean instant defeat.

Thomas and Dennis Rodman were pressuring down on Earvin, raking and ripping at the ball, smacking him in the face. He lifted his eyes for a split second and saw A. C. Green streaking down to the floor.

Earvin faked a forward lunge, then reared back and took the ball in both hands, ending his dribble. As the defenders swarmed over his body, he muscled a seventy-foot pass to A.C. Three and a half seconds were left in the game when Green caught the ball on the run. Bill Laimbeer, all two hundred and sixty malevolent pounds of him, was thundering down on his heels. Two seconds were left on the clock as A.C. laid the ball softly over the rim. Another moment that I will never forget as long as I live.

Only then did I have the conviction that our Mission would be accomplished.

An instant later there was no more time left on the clock. Our dream had come true. Not only the first back-to-back wins in nearly two decades of NBA competition, but a total of five championships in the decade, the most of any pro team in any sport.

Afterward, as always, I reviewed the game on videotape. I listened over and over again to Dick Stockton, the great play-by-play announcer for CBS, as he counted down the final two seconds: "This is a moment they will remember for the rest of their lives. It took three seven-game series to get the job done. And they did it. The first team in nineteen years to win back-to-back championships. A TRULY SIGNIFICANT ACHIEVEMENT!"

Three days later I was talking with Byron Scott, who had made some of the most crucial shots of the playoffs for us. He told me, "I've never been more exhausted physically, mentally, or spiritually in my life."

"That's exactly the way you should feel," I told him. "It took twenty-four games, more than a quarter of an entire regular season, including three seven-game series, and every bit of energy and effort you had to win the greatest prize.

"And"—I held up my right hand with the thumb and forefinger a fraction of an inch apart—"we only won it by *that much*. It took all you had, and all the entire team could give, to win just barely in the closing two seconds of a drive that began in training camp—ten months ago.

"This is what a Mission is all about—endurance."

What Byron got for his endurance, his focus, and his hard work was the privilege of knowing that what he did really counted, really mattered. He earned that satisfaction because he committed to something bigger than himself—a team. He helped that team reach a level of accomplishment that very few teams—in any field—will ever achieve.

"The privilege of a lifetime is being who you are."
—*Joseph Campbell*

The only way to get through challenges is to lock in on a Mission, a desired state of being. Like Frank Rodstrom, J. I. Rodale, or Michael Fuchs, you must be willing to raise the stakes, get your objective clear, collect your firepower, and follow through doggedly until the job is done.

Time-Out

For the first time in the cycle of winning, the team has the opportunity to take two positive steps in a row as Mastery is wagered and the ante is upped. The very opposite of the Choke—where confidence is denied—Anteing Up claims an unbeatable excellence and defies others to challenge it. Instead of winning a championship, the total focus is on being a championship team—becoming historically significant and leaving footprints. Upping the ante often costs colossal exertion of effort and endurance.

10

Core Cracking

"Fate leads him who follows it,
and drags him who resists."
—*Plutarch*

"When you cannot make up your mind which of
two evenly balanced courses of action
you should take—choose the bolder."
—*General W. J. Slim*

T he three-day whirlwind of the 1992 NBA draft had just ended. New York Knicks president Dave Checketts and Ernie Grunfeld, Vice President of Player Personnel for the Knicks, had made two promising deals for the future of the Knicks: acquiring Rolando Blackman and drafting Hubert Davis, the nephew of ex-NBA great Walter Davis. Rolando had been burning defenders, consistently scoring around twenty points a game, for over a decade. Hubert had an outside shot very similar to the one that had earned his Uncle Walter the NBA's Rookie of the Year award in 1978.

After all the frenzy of the draft, I was looking forward to some peaceful time with my family. I flew back into Los Angeles on June 26th, gliding in on an eastern approach, a flight path I'd ridden thousands of times.

It was a familiar landscape, but I was seeing it with different eyes. First there was the Coachella Valley desert, and Palm Springs—where Chris and I courted and spent our wonderful first nights together, where the Lakers met for training camp for so many years, renewing our allegiances to one another at the beginning of each new season.

After the interconnected string of suburbs came the vista of Los Angeles, a mass of several million people who are gathered together and yet are not really together. Neighborhoods with aqua-blue pools in rambling backyards. Neighborhoods strewn with scorched piles of cinder block rubble and heat-twisted steel beams, the aftermath of the 1992 L.A. riots.

Just before the wheels unfolded from the plane's belly and wings in final descent, we passed over the Forum, the Roman-style rotunda ringed with white columns where I had played out almost a quarter century of basketball dramas. Memories flooded back. Throngs of thousands crowding the parking lot, waiting for us to guarantee back-to-back championships. Crazy fans tailing my car for miles, forcing me to dodge down side streets like a character in a Raymond Chandler novel. The series of miracle shots that Kareem, Magic, James, Coop, Silk, and all the others made, the high-fives and hugs that capped big wins. The incredible moment of our first championship, when I stood out on the court remembering that championship look on every face.

I remembered the time in 1985 at my fortieth birthday party when Cooper had collapsed, faking a painful knee injury, writhing on the floor, mutter-

ing "It popped, Coach!" Just as my jaw hit the
floor, he got up, grinning like a bandit, and moon-
walked out of the room before I chased him down
the boulevard.

Then a really sentimental thought crossed my
mind: wouldn't it be great to get all of the Laker
players, coaches, owners, trainers, and their families together? Two decades' worth of L.A. Lakers.
All of us together just one more time. Remembering the family barbecues. The old videos. Our
theme songs. The championship banners. All those
celebrations.

"A man is not old
until regrets take the
place of dreams."
—*John Barrymore*

Looking out the jetliner's window, my mind
painted a picture of champagne bubbling out from
all the columns and foaming down the sides of the
building. Memories flashed: the team Christmas
party where our tree had been decorated with
jockstraps, Ace bandages, and spools of trainer's
tape. The season when our top rookie had arrived
for a road game packing two left shoes. Kareem's
last regular season game, when we had all pitched
in and given him a Rolls-Royce and a rocking
chair.

My Laker memories are indelible. I got to be part
of something that meant a whole lot to the people
of Los Angeles. Those Forum columns were a
magic ring, an affirmation of life's high possibilities, a boundary where special things were made to
happen. They surely happened for me. My own
stature and recognition grew, thanks to players
like Kareem and Earvin and to so many other great
people who gave their all, until I was eventually
surrounded by rewards beyond my dreams.

But not all my memories connected with the
Forum are happy. Some undeniably painful things
happened there, and some of the worst of them

came late and off the court. The aura of the Lakers will glow in my heart forever, but the struggle and conflict that go into attaining competitive superiority sometimes leave people combative and wounded. In the end, betrayal and regrets can threaten to spoil part of the legacy of grandeur and victory.

During my last two seasons with the Lakers, some events were deeply wrenching. They were part of the inevitable cycles that drive growth and change in teams. *Renewal always begins with destruction, a cracking of the Core Covenant, and its inner center of people. Renewal begins with pain.* The key is guiding the pain in the direction of renewal. If the coming apart is handled unaware, it just leads to more useless pain.

I had as tough a time keeping up with change as anyone else. I lost some touch with the growth cycle of some of the players, and it showed in my communication. People never stay the same. In the case of the Lakers, a time came when some key people stopped being effective in their roles and the core could not hold together.

Cores crumble for other reasons, too. Drives and motivations shift direction or intensity. Alliances wither and regroup. Antiteam behavior, dormant or held in check, lashes loose. Whatever the reason, the team no longer offers security or camaraderie. Instead it becomes a center for bitterness.

Take the case of my good friend Robert Towne. Towne is an Oscar-winning screenwriter who gave us the great film classic *Chinatown*. Everyone wanted a sequel, with Jack Nicholson again playing the unforgettable, small-change PI Jake Gittes, so Robert, and his close friends Nicholson and producer-actor Bob Evans, were set to do one, called

"When you come to a fork in the road, take it."
—*Yogi Berra*

The Two Jakes. Evans was to play the key role of the second Jake. Painfully, however, Towne reached the conclusion that Evans couldn't carry the part. Production was suddenly shut down, which literally cost millions. What followed was a protracted struggle which no one really won. Evans lost, because he was ultimately replaced. Towne lost, because when production started again, he was off the team. Nicholson lost, because taking on the combined roles of director, unofficial producer, and lead actor added up to the toughest struggle of his career. The studio and the public both lost, because *The Two Jakes* wasn't really a worthy successor to *Chinatown.* And, in the process, a quarter century of friendships and working relationships connecting the people at the film's original core were shredded.

When people go off in their own individual directions as the core team of *The Two Jakes* or the Lakers did, the core has lost its sense of leadership. A friend of Chris's and mine named Dr. Lew Richfield is a psychotherapist and professional team-mender in California. He specializes in welding together everything from corporations to mergers. "Teams break," Dr. Lew is convinced, "when they don't have a goal or the goals aren't clearly defined by the leaders. Goals have to be firmly entrenched, otherwise people begin to operate as independent entrepreneurs in a system that really needs cooperative work."

"You do not merely want to be considered just the best of the best. You want to be considered the only ones who do what you do."
—*Jerry Garcia of The Grateful Dead*

> ### Riles' Rule of the
> ### Inappropriate Entrepreneur
> The Inappropriate Entrepreneur arises out of a
> cracked core like a vulture. Out for himself, he feeds
> off the carrion of the dying team for anything he can
> get.

While you cannot fall in love with your goals,
they can help keep a lid on selfish behavior. An
untogether team is a case study in selfishness. The
Inappropriate Entrepreneur comes down with a
fresh case of the Disease of Me when playing offense and is a virtuoso at Cover Your Ass on defense. In *Vanguard Management,* James O'Toole
wrote that a deadened corporate culture gives itself away by the amount of time people spend
cranking out memos, covering their backsides.

To take it further, you can spot a disintegrating
team by how much fear drives or surrounds the
contact that takes place between its members.

Someone who works in one of New York's greatest hospitals described to me recently how staff
insecurity there has grown both rampant and
toxic, up and down the corridors. As funds shrink
and positions are slashed, new managers can be
sure that veteran employees hate them. Staff
members are torn between getting the hell out or
backstabbing and undercutting their teammates in
order to hang on to a job. Many actually carry
microcassette recorders at all times, openly tape-
recording any conversation touching on job performance or team goals. Practically anything they
should be openly talking about to renew the team
is instead logged for future possible use in some

lawsuit or formal complaint. And the people taking names and notes think anybody not armed with their own recorder is a moron. This so-called team is deader than the corpses down in the fridges of the hospital's autopsy room.

What a contrast this un-team is to a dynamic, seventeen-physician group I know in California called the Kerlan-Jobe Orthopedic Clinic. It's headed by Dr. Robert Kerlan, one of the great figures in sports medicine. Although slowed by age and crippling arthritis, he explains the dynamism of surgical teamwork with nimble vitality. Dr. Kerlan says the surgeon is in absolute charge of the operating suite, but the surgeon is really a player-coach not a boss. "A surgical team," says Dr. Kerlan, "consists of five principal roles: the surgeon, the assistant surgeon, the anesthetist, the scrub nurse, and the run nurse. An anesthetist can be as important as or even more important to the outcome than the surgeon if the patient is in a shaky situation.

"Adversity causes some men to break; others to break records."
—*William A. Ward*

"Generally, assistants will have worked with surgeons over a long period of time for the same surgical procedure, and the assistant will learn the surgeon's moves and body language. An effective assistant anticipates and doesn't need to be told each time where to place the retractor, senses how to keep the wound clean and clear, and knows where to tie off a bleeding vessel. Some scrub nurses do a great job in anticipating when they hand off instruments. Like basketball players who know to pass the ball, a great scrub nurse gets high marks for assists in this league."

A cracked core and a together core—and both in the most distinguished circles of advanced medicine. The only difference is a matter of attitude.

Only attitude. But, if you had a major orthopedic operation coming up, would you rather have it in that legendary hospital where today a paranoid staff lurks around, tape-recording possible job threats . . . or in one where enthusiastic collaboration is a badge of honor?

Do legends—hospitals or people—have a lifespan? No doubt they do. The greatness of an athletic dynasty can carry it for ten years. Perhaps it is truly great for five years and maybe it rides on its laurels for another five.

Because of all the changes in technology, global competitors (and copycats), or Wall Street hammering for more and more profits, a successful company may go through the same cycle in only five years, not ten. That happened in the early nineties to several high-growth computer makers that had rocketed to industry stardom in the late eighties, when low-end price competitors challenged fine product lines long before it was expected. As Peter Drucker wrote recently, "the most probable assumption is that no currently working business theory will be valid 10 years hence—at least not without major modifications." So any company that's great today, and also great a decade from now, is likely to have become a very different place in the interim. That puts a huge premium on embracing and mastering change, on tackling something that scares people to death.

I was once invited to talk to the managers of the Marina City Club, a huge, upscale condo complex in Marina Del Rey, the yacht capital of Los Angeles. It was a great, prestigious place to work, but ownership of the complex had changed hands. Thirty-five managers all feared the new owner would replace them and put them out of a job.

"Success is never final."
—*Winston Churchill*

Obsession with that worry caused the level of service around the complex to go to hell.

"You're going about this all wrong," I said. "Sure, there may be tremendous change. Or maybe none at all. But the only thing for you to do is embrace the change. Approach the new owner and say, 'Here we are! We know how to take care of business. What is your philosophy? What is your plan? We'll get behind it.' " It pleased me to know that my talk helped. It helped change their perspective and made them more ready to sign up to the new Covenant.

In the vain hope of clinging to a false security, change always takes the rap. *The Winner Within* knows that security is always imaginary . . . deceptive . . . unattainable. But if you can't have security in dealing with change, what can you have? What will pull you through when a Core Covenant is cracking? Spiritually, you have to have faith, especially faith in self. Physically and mentally, there's no replacement for stamina.

"Nothing so fatiguing as the eternal hanging on of an uncompleted task."
—*William James*

In a way, you see a miniature version of the Core Covenant cracking on a team when its stamina is sapped in a competitive contest. Basketball is a game of conditioning and fatigue. That's why I believe in practicing a team to train when it's exhausted. For a pro-basketball team, at the fortieth minute, fatigue jars the starters, and patterns and strategies start to collapse. When the pattern breaks down, the individual must rely on judgment. If you don't have stamina, you'll never have the presence of mind to exercise judgment.

Fatigue makes cowards of us all—individuals and organizations—and cowardice is an archenemy of sound judgment. Just as players and teams suffer fatigue, so do companies. Businesses don't understand how *competitive fatigue* can drag them down and crack the big picture of the Core Covenant. A good coach can spot fatigue in a player in a flash. With sharpened observation, a good manager, too, can spot competitive fatigue in a company or a business plan:

Riles' Symptoms for Fatigue Disease

• Does the game plan feel like a cage? "If we can't compete on price . . . and we can't compete on quality or innovation . . . what *can* we compete on?"
• Do the opponents appear out of focus? Do they sometimes feel bigger than life . . . and at other times look like lucky simpletons?
• Is there a falloff in the measures of competitive *effort?* (Effort, mind you, not results. A winning team or business can often slide by for a long time talent-rich, while it has really lost the will to win, the determination to try harder.)
• Do team members disagree about who the competition is or how to beat them?
• Are leaders spending more time settling petty personal disputes than upholding the key principles and plans?

You beat fatigue by continually reexamining and reaffirming your game plan. You beat it by reality-checking your opponents constantly. You beat fatigue by adjusting your game plan to the continual personal growth and perception changes of the individuals on your team. Most of all, you beat it by superior stamina and the mental training that lets you be more alert to the world around you than your competitors are.

The fatigue that the Lakers knew in 1989–1990 was beyond the fatigue of body and mind; it was the aimless fatigue of spirit.

The Los Angeles Lakers eventually drifted into a case study in Core Cracking. It wasn't the descent from championship peaks or even my personal need to move along that troubled me most. It was how a significant team could transform itself into a collection of individuals that practiced the same dissension we had so often mocked in other teams.

As the Lakers began our 1988–1989 season, it was without a compelling theme. It was Kareem's last season, and we wanted to send him out a winner—we talked about winning one for the Big Fella.

In Earvin's recent book, *My Life*, he portrays Kareem through the eyes of a player: "In addition to being the most intelligent athlete I've ever known, he's also the most mysterious. I've never understood Kareem . . . maybe that's not surprising for a guy who barely spoke to me during my first five years on his team." And that's true. For a long time they had no personal relationship at all. So you can imagine how much emotion Kareem showed most of the less-significant players. A thin slice above zero. In turn, they called him—behind his back, of course—"the brother from another planet."

Nonetheless, Kareem was a leader. He was the patriarch. Like most patriarchs, he hated disruptions and distractions. He wanted tranquillity and really understood the difference between winning and fighting. It disgusted him when teammates aired petty differences. He kept them in line, mostly because they were deathly afraid of cross-

"Even if you're on the right track, you'll get run over if you just sit there."
—*Will Rogers*

ing him. But respect based on fear eventually turns into resentment.

In the history of the game, Kareem was not the only superstar to have a problem with his own teammates. Wilt Chamberlain literally wrote the book *Nobody Loves Goliath.*

Riles' Rule of the Departing Warrior

When the do-or-die gladiator hangs up his sword, the fear and awe that marked the team's respect of him during his reign may turn to resentment and turmoil. The Warrior's departure may throw his own team off-balance on leaving, as much as his aggressiveness earlier undercut the team's opponents on the field.

Compounding the situation, there were commercially sponsored plans to turn his final season into an orchestrated Farewell Tour. It was deserved that one of the longest and most fruitful NBA careers should be capped in a special way. But twenty-six long, lavish pre-game ceremonies on the road wore down on already-thin tolerance levels—including probably Kareem's own. We gave him a Rolls-Royce, paid for by his own team and delivered on the last game of the regular season.

After that last game, there was a telling locker room incident. Kareem always rushed into the shower first. He loved to pull practical jokes on the other players when they were still showering—hiding wallets, switching clothes, embarrassing them in a hundred different ways. So, as the fitting climax of his tribute night, they paid homage to his practical joking. The trainer handed each player a pair of scissors, and as a team, they all cut his jeans to ribbons. Kareem tried a laugh, but the look that came out of his eyes was pure death-ray. The look was not about the cost of the jeans. It was about authority.

Of course, the events revolving around Kareem weren't to blame. Lack of tolerance was the problem, and it was a problem that would build more and more as the core of the team got older and experienced change.

"Everybody wants to go to heaven, but nobody wants to die."
—*Joe Louis*

In spite of distractions, the Lakers had a great season, cut a new notch in the record book, and competed for a third consecutive championship. At fifty-seven and twenty-five in the regular season, we were among the NBA's top three teams. In the playoffs we went undefeated all the way through the Western Conference Finals. No other team had ever scored eleven straight postseason wins. It looked for all the world like we would notch yet another championship. And, as in the 1988 campaign, we again had a long layoff while we waited for an Eastern Conference winner to emerge. Once again we took off for a few days of seclusion and renewal in Santa Barbara. Then, as we contemplated our chances of becoming the only undefeated team in NBA playoff history, Thunderbolts struck.

Sometimes the human body just breaks down under extended pressure, despite the best stamina training. A team that reaches the championship round plays the equivalent of one and a half seasons in one year. We had one of the oldest rosters in the league, and we were entering our third straight finals. The odds for disaster on our team were building.

Byron Scott, who had been averaging almost twenty points a game, tore a hamstring muscle on the eve of our series opener. Despite our efforts to adjust, on June 6th, Detroit took game one, 109–97. On June 8th, two minutes into the third quarter of game two, Earvin pulled up with the same injury that had ended the playoffs for Byron. With the snap of two hamstrings, the best starting back court in the NBA was hobbled and gone for the series. Our reserves put up a great struggle, losing by just three points.

I remember the sight of Earvin sitting in the shower after game two, with water cascading down his face, sobbing in total misery, knowing that he was now out. If there had been a sword to fall on, I swear he would have bloodied the shower room.

In game three, the Big Fella almost carried the day. His twenty-four points and thirteen rebounds was his top performance of the season and among the finer moments of his twenty-year career, but came up four points short. James Worthy stepped up in game four with forty points, but not enough to stop Detroit from wrapping up the series with a sweep.

It was a real disappointment to get swept in the finals after having won eleven consecutive games. It was probably the most disappointing playoff loss we ever had, on the verge of being a "three-peater." Afterward, I had a premonition that I would be entering my final season as a Laker.

When that next year began, the knowledge that Kareem was gone left an empty feeling. There was also the unanswered question of whether we could make it without him. It was the start of a new culture. When Kareem was with the team, he knew what I was doing, what was in the team's best interest, even if it meant putting up with my traits and occasional flak. With Kareem gone, the order and structure of the team was destined to change.

I tried to overcome the disappointment and emptiness in our first team meeting at training camp in Hawaii. "Why did we win more games in the NBA in one decade than anybody else has ever done?" I looked Earvin in the eye and posed the question: "Was it because of you? Or was it West and Buss and team management? Was it the coaching? Was it Kareem?"

Magic stood up and said, smiling, "Riles, we know what you're trying to do. You're trying to come up with another theme. *You're* trying to tell us that we won all these championships in the eighties because of Kareem. Well, maybe we did. But we know what you're doing. You're trying to fire us up." And then Earvin looked back at his buddies for effect, while the grin spread across his face. "The fellas and me were talking about this last night. We guessed what you were going to say. But the question isn't whether we can win without Kareem in the nineties—it's whether *you* can *coach* without him."

We had a great laugh. Unfortunately, laughs were few and far between. The record shows that we were the dominant regular-season team that year, with the best win/loss record in the NBA. But the record doesn't show how the core of the Lakers fragmented. As a decade of sustained high achievement came to its close, the core of Laker greatness cracked. We disconnected from the realities of teamwork. And here's how.

While a business career can stretch across four or five decades, an NBA career—for the lucky few who climb that high on the competitive pyramid—

averages around three years. Along with thrills, fantastic paychecks, and accolades, players can experience a crushing amount of personal insecurity.

Among core players, two were having rough years in 1989–1990. One was younger; the other older.

The younger one may have been tentative about testing himself physically and developing injuries. Whatever the cause, his game was out of sync. He had always been a bit of a rebel. Because his numbers were down in shooting percentage, point production, rebounds, assists, and in drawing fouls, I had to be hard on him. We needed those numbers back. At a highly emotional team meeting, he told me, "Every time I talk to you, you throw it right back in my face."

I said, "You're right. When you tell me that you'll come to practice and work hard, and then you don't do it, I'm going to throw it back in your face. When you don't support the spirit of the team and don't show the attitude of being a winner, I'm going to throw it back in your face. But you don't want to hear the truth anymore. You want me to sugarcoat everything."

The older player was facing retirement. The speed and force that had been his stock in trade was disappearing. Psychologists say that retirement is one of the most stressful events in a person's entire life. People must mourn retirement "death," the death of a role, before they can forge a new identity. He faced his imminent career "death" with a classic reaction—denial. He disconnected from the realities of the situation. He blamed coaching decisions. But I wasn't his enemy. Father Time was.

Both troubled players were losing chunks of playing time to a newcomer. In the summer of 1988, the Lakers had signed on a brilliant talent named Orlando Woolridge. He arrived at a time when the core began to weaken, and gave us plenty of exciting basketball. His long-stride slashes to the basket were spectacular. I still recall with amazement the lethal dunk shot he unloaded right over the top, between the outstretched arms of seven-foot-seven Manute Bol. However, a few of the Lakers resented Woolridge and perceived him to be selfish, even as he unselfishly tried to help shore up the core.

"Instead of loving your enemies, treat your friends a little better."
—*Ed Howe*

That was our team's state of mind. We had the best record in the NBA, so we were obviously doing a few things right. But for some players, team success didn't make up for their own personal roles shrinking. On the court, we were kicking ass. In the locker room, we were a team distanced and apart.

The cracks in the core became a wide-open split in the middle of January 1990. One of the older players went behind my back to management to air his grievances. All of a sudden the Forum had become a house divided.

Children learn that when one parent says they can't have an ice cream cone, it sometimes works to go find the other parent and ask again. Sooner or later, the parents have to catch on and speak with one voice. If they don't, a three-way battle of the wills is going to follow.

I had had a long history with Laker management. Most of them had worked their way up from roles as players, and we had a good understanding. So this was a completely new situation for me.

In spite of our then being the winningest team in

the NBA, management responded to player complaints by doing something they had never done before in the ten years of our coach/management relationship. When someone from the front office stepped into a team meeting and undercut my authority, the whole situation came to a volatile head.

Riles' Rule of Oneness

Management must speak with one voice. The chain of command must run from players to coach, from coach to manager, from manager to owner. When it doesn't, management itself becomes a peripheral opponent to the team's Mission.

Management should have told the player, "This is something you've got to settle with Riley." Breaking the chain of command was like letting a kid pit one parent against the other—and at a time when we had the best record in the NBA and were in the process of being selected Team of the Decade.

When she studied for certification as a Marriage and Family Counselor, my wife, Chris, learned that patients sometimes draw great benefits from switching professionals. It's not that the new one is smarter than the old one. It's just that people sometimes respond best to fresh viewpoints and techniques. Over ten years the Lakers may have had their fill of me. As the team's core aged, one key member already gone, others either in decline or approaching it, my tactics and speeches lost some of their edge. I wasn't as successful at changing players' minds, sharpening their focus, or helping people get out of themselves and with the team.

No matter how high we had reached in the past, by 1990 we were a team with no choice but to embrace change. One by one, we all followed Kareem out the door.

There will always be painful moments in a team's transition from greatness to mediocrity to rebuilding. We tasted some of that pain when we bombed out in the second round of the 1990 playoffs. In the playoffs, a team's character either pulls it through or pulls it under. We were wearied by the dissension. Earvin, unwilling to give in, all but carried us on his back. It wasn't enough to overcome a younger, hungrier, happier, ascendant Phoenix Suns team.

In the case of the Lakers, change ran its course in a way that left bitter residues. Insecurity became resentment; resentment became toxicity. But change cannot be sidestepped. It is up to *The Winner Within* to find, in the words of an old prayer, the courage to change what you can, the serenity to know what you can't, and the wisdom to know the difference.

The evolution of the people on the team eventually makes the core crack and nothing can change that. Because a basketball career is brief, that evolution will show itself more rapidly than in a business career, but the processes are the same.

The decline of the Lakers was nobody's fault—not mine, not management's, not the players'.* It was the phenomenon of winning playing itself out. It was simply time for us to sit in the same room,

"Character is destiny."
—*Heraclitus*

*What's going on now in Los Angeles is the final stage of the process, and everyone there is paying the price for the winning of the eighties.

look each other in the eye, and say, "We had a great run. All of us. Now, instead of wounding each other, let's say thanks and goodbye."

It took me six weeks to decide to leave the Lakers. I wanted the transition to be as smooth and classy as possible. In the meantime, anonymous and not-so-anonymous comments began to surface. They validated what I was thinking: "It's okay. It's painful, but it's time for moving on."

That realization nudged me out the door. And what was the greatest irony of my leaving? I had just been voted Coach of the Year and Coach of the Decade.

Form changes, spirit lasts. The form, the organization, the platform may change, but *The Winner Within* can always recapture the spirit. The spirit can light anywhere. It can be brought to any team. All it needs is a portal. *The Winner Within* can be that portal.

Time-Out

Veterans of greatness can and should uphold the legacy that their team performance has earned. They must also recognize that nothing is forever, that the core will crack. When the core cracks, *The Winner Within* doesn't lose all gains: certain parts of the past can be made a part of oneself and form the basis for future growth, but the team as a whole has a different destiny. Because of age, deteriorating ability, or other personal reasons, some will leave the team. The glory days are gone. The team-breaking patterns, which have been subdued and held in check, but never totally obliterated, will finally lash out. This is the toxic and terminal phase of Core Cracking. Core Cracking is a realist's recognition that the cycle of change cannot be sidestepped.

11

Moving On

"If one advances confidently in the direction
of his dreams, and endeavors to live the life
which he has imagined, he will meet with
success unexpected in common hours."
—Henry David Thoreau

"Faith is the substance of things hoped for,
the evidence of things not seen."
—Hebrews 11:1

Once the Riley family had decided to leave Los Angeles and head east, we had to face moving twenty years' worth of material and emotional possessions—house, family, friends, and home.

August 26th, 1991, it was 99 degrees in Greenwich, Connecticut, with 90 percent humidity. An awful day to move into a new house. Men in dust-streaked white overalls were maneuvering their trucks in the driveway, walking in and out, stacking boxes in every corner of every room. All of us were dripping perspiration.

The first thing to get put in place was the piano. In all the mayhem and the heat, we would intermittently hear our son, James, who was then six, sitting on the piano bench and producing clusters of musical notes. Through the next two weeks we kept hearing little piano chords coming together, but whenever we walked into the living room, he would stop what he was doing and say, "Not yet. It's not finished."

Finally one night he played his little song for us. It was an astonishing achievement for a six-year-old's mind and fingers. Two tight verses. Harmony, lyrics, and a rhythm to it.

"Good-bye, my friend
Good-bye, my friend
I hope I'll see you
again real soon
And when we are together
It will be the happiest day."
—*James Riley*

Our daughter, Elisabeth, asked, "James, what is it?"

"It's called 'Good-bye, My Friend,'" he said. "It's for Steven. I miss him and I want to record it and send it to him."

Chris and I sat there, feeling this wonderful pride in our son, mixed with a letting-go of all the hurt that had come with uprooting our lives. It was an unbelievable moment. A kid got to a piano and wrote a song and put it all very poignantly into perspective: "Good-bye, My Friend." His buddy Steven stood for Jerry Buss, Earvin Johnson, the Lakers, Bill and Solveig, Steve and Holly, Robert and Luisa, Tom and Claire, Los Angeles, everything left behind.

It's no coincidence that a couple of our friends had also made a big leap in the middle of their careers and had done so for the better. This kind of change has been happening to more and more people.

You first heard about Steve and Holly Chabre in Chapter 4, and how Holly whipped the Thunderbolt of breast cancer and complex invasive surgery. Steve Chabre has been a great friend over the years, and he is himself a great example of a businessperson who has moved onward to a fresh career cycle.

Over a decade, Steve had risen to become chief

operating officer of Dailey and Associates in Los Angeles—a $200 million advertising agency. But he knew that he wanted to do something different, so he set up his own marketing firm and spent the first year transforming the marketing program of the Lakers into a huge success. The big skill Steve learned in moving on was how an outsider could still be a team player. Steve is now President and Chief Executive Officer of all of Michael Jackson's business enterprises, including a 2700-acre California ranch.

"When an executive transitions to an independent career," Steve says, "you have to learn that the independent adviser in a service business— such as a consultant, an accountant, or an attorney—must often be the consummate team player with their clients, perhaps *more* so than somebody on the official 'inside' roster. Entrepreneurial outsiders have to try extra hard to present themselves as team members because they don't have the traditional authority structure to help them."

The outside aide has to become a *peripheral contributor* and not peripheral opponent. That's what Steve Chabre has moved on to after a life in the world of big business: an all-star career as a peripheral contributor par excellence.

A second acquaintance who has made the Big Change with great success is Dr. Lew Richfield, whom I mentioned in the last chapter. If you had never met Dr. Lew and talked with him on the phone, you'd swear he was forty-two—*max.* However, Dr. Lew is about to celebrate his seventieth birthday. He's an avid golfer, he's just taken up horseback riding, and he has written a couple of books on aging and relationships. Still, along the way to becoming assistant to the chairman of a

"I'm no good in permanent positions. My feet go to sleep."
—*Kevin Costner, as detective Frank Farmer in* The Bodyguard

$140 million company, Dr. Lew missed one particular credential. He'd never gone to college. Until he was forty-seven, that is.

When he turned forty-five, Dr. Lew became a volunteer worker for a suicide prevention center because he felt he owed something to the community. Professionals encouraged him to make something of it in a formal way. His wife, Gloria, cheered him on to go for it. After mulling it over, the house was sold and both he and she were in college together, living in a little apartment like a couple of kids.

Dr. Lew now has three degrees (including a Ph.D.), a license in California as a family therapist, and a successful practice in West Los Angeles. The internship required three thousand hours of practical work, under supervision, before he could sit for the state boards in California. Chris actually helped train Dr. Lew for his new profession—in what must have been one of the great visual role reversals of all time. Even then Dr. Lew looked like the classic, fatherly psychotherapist—beard and all. His rite of passage took six years, making him fifty-two by the time he was finished with just the preliminaries for his new profession.

Why go through all of that? "If you go to a baseball game, sitting in the stands, hoping a ball is going to get hit to you," Dr. Lew says, "you're going to wait a very long time. You've got to get out into the field." But you must have the confidence you can win. "Visualize exactly what it's going to look like—your office, your clothes, your car, everything that is wrapped up in your goal," Dr. Lew believes. "And then you've got to get it off the front burner, but keep it plainly fixed in your mind

"When you make a major career change, there has to be some kind of connection. I remember a Beverly Hills attorney who wanted to become a potato farmer in Oregon. Well, there's a guy who's born to lose."
—Dr. Lew Richfield

and in your heart. Follow the signs that lead to your goal."

The renewals I have experienced have usually moved me around to different places and organizations, but that need not always be the case. Moving on *does* require a new Core Covenant and sometimes a new core team or team Mission if a person attempts rebirth within the same organization. In short, all the conditions must be in place to enable an Innocent Climb such as described in Chapter 1. It is certainly harder to "move on" while you stay in the same place, because all of the cues and relationships are there to reinforce the old behaviors, but it certainly can be done. For example, Sears is shedding its catalog operations and will present its financial services business in a public offering. A whole different vision of the Sears business is taking shape, as this company moves along the road to becoming a more sharply focused retail merchandiser. The employees at the GM Fremont plant became some of the most skilled automotive workers in America when the plant transformed itself into NUMMI. It just requires a new Innocent Climb.

But sometimes "moving on" means literally moving on. "Follow the signs," said Dr. Lew. Well, I was now following the signs that led to New York! Before I landed there, plenty of people asked me, "What is it going to be like in New York?" And I always answered, "I know one thing. It might be exhilaratingly bad or it might be exhilaratingly good. But I know it's going to be exhilarating."

"Between two evils, I always pick the one I never tried before."
—*Mae West*

> ### Riles' Rule of Change
> The changes in your life aren't always the ones you hoped for. But they can usually help you grow. I say this: when you face a fork in the road, step on the exhilarator!

The changes in my life have not always gone in the directions I hoped for, but they have indeed always taken me to places and situations where I could learn and grow. One summer morning in 1963 I got up at six and drove from Schenectady, New York, to Lexington, Kentucky, where I was a complete fish out of water, yet blessed with one of the greatest coaches in basketball history, none other than Adolph Rupp. Then the NBA draft brought me to the San Diego Rockets—not the Boston Celtics or the Cincinnati Royals, as I wanted it to. But there I met the woman who would become my wife, and forever remain my wife, in spite of all the financial and emotional insecurities that went along with being a young, struggling player on a cellar-dwelling team. Then I was sent to Portland, and seemed on my way out of the league, when a near-fluke decision by the Lakers put me on a team that was to become the winningest group in the history of pro sports. Then, after being cut and having to learn how to dismiss my bitterness and envy, I found myself doing the production and broadcasting work that drew me back into the Laker family. With every one of those moves and changes, there was fear. With each, I scarcely appreciated its importance when it happened. But somehow every step led me to a better place.

When your core cracks, you have two alternatives: either to create a new team and Core Covenant by initiating change where you are, or to move on, as Lew Richfield, Steve Chabre, and I did. My job at the New York Knicks, along with Knicks president Dave Checketts and vice president of player personnel Ernie Grunfeld, has been to build a new setting, a new culture. To do that, I brought with me the lessons I had learned in my basketball career from sixteen different coaches— some of them masters—hundreds of teammates, including several all-time greats, and from my experiences leading the greatest pro-sports team of its era.

The 1991–1992 season brought the Knicks a fantastic turnaround in team fortunes. Team growth that took years of trial-and-error with the Lakers got telescoped into an incredibly short span. We achieved the team's best season in nineteen years and built the base to do even better the year that followed.

The Knicks had started the season with a single goal: to become the hardest-working, best-conditioned, toughest, most professional, unselfish, and disliked team in the NBA.

"It is only in our decisions that we are important."
—*Jean-Paul Sartre*

Learning from all the Thunderbolt injuries that hit the Lakers in the 1980s, we brought on Greg Brittenham, probably the best weight and strength coach in the league. We spent a lot of time before and after each practice warding off potential Thunderbolts through weight and flexibility training, cardiovascular fitness, diet and nutrition counseling. With the demands to come, no one would break down for lack of proper conditioning.

All year long, no big-time injuries hit us. We were the healthiest team in the league. Only once was a starter not available at game time, and that was because of a totally positive kind of Thunderbolt. Mark Jackson missed the December 28th game when his wife, Desiree, gave birth to Mark A. Jackson II.

The expectations the Knicks faced in my first season were jacked up sky-high. We posted a terrific pre-season. Lots of season tickets were sold, lots of sponsors came on board. Then, after the first two games of the year, which we lost, the old doubts came out. The big balloon of new-coach hype was losing air.

But the start was a blessing. I told the team, losing is just as much a part of the NBA as winning. You simply have to know how to deal with it. The overreaction to those two losses showed how much fear, doubt, worry, and negativity were in the organization.

I was already too positively psyched for the Knicks to buckle. Back when I had resigned from the Lakers, I had jogged on the beach every day of that whole summer. As I ran, I imagined myself becoming the New York Knicks coach. I knew, given the team's up-and-down track record, that change was likely. Turnover among NBA coaches is brutal.

My "jog-a-logues" got real specific. I even thought out my conversations with the players. I knew how I was going to challenge Patrick Ewing and Charles Oakley to help build an unselfish core. How I would talk to each player, to try to motivate them away from the way they were being perceived. How I'd underline pride, dignity, and integrity to bring the group together. That was my vision of the future, my own personal Mission Motivation. And then, on May 1st, 1991, it came

"If you do not have some bad loans, you are not in business."
—*Paul Volcker*

true. I was named the head coach of the New York Knicks.

When I sat down and talked to Patrick Ewing and his wife, Rita, I told him about how I'd spent a whole summer envisioning it. How I also visualized, one day, a parade going down Broadway, with confetti snowing down in that canyon of skyscrapers. People cheering from the curbs, wearing T-shirts boasting: KNICK POWER—BACK TO BACK. And I told him, "One day it's going to happen to this franchise. I don't care what somebody else thinks, I believe it's gonna happen."

A tremendous share of credit for the Knicks' reemergence goes to team president Dave Checketts, who renegotiated contracts to get the team under the salary cap and made our team-building trades possible. But, in an emotional sense, the reemergence began with Patrick Ewing.

There was a time when people thought Patrick only cared about one guy. But deep down, what Patrick wanted more than anything else was to be part of a winning team, surrounded by players whose abilities complemented his own. Through frustrating years of unmet promises and revolving-door coaches and managers—whose number ran into double boxcars over five years—the evidence told Patrick that the Knicks might never get it together. Since he had to endure the misery of expending his world-class skills in vain, there's no wonder that the comfort of money looked like the best medicine.

At my first meeting with Patrick I said, "Every time there's a new general manager, a new coach, they come and tell you, 'We're gonna get you the players, we're gonna get you this, we're gonna get you that.' It never happens. Why am I any different?"

I pledged that this management team was willing to go further than any past one. I also told him that, as a result, the pressure on him would be unmatched because he'd be expected to stand as the core of a championship team. We were committed to bringing in players who wanted to win, I said, and to getting rid of those who didn't: "If there's a player on this team who thinks his big-money contract guarantees him a position, and if that player doesn't produce, he's making the biggest mistake of his life."

Patrick was hearing news. Big-contract players rarely get traded. Why should another club pick up an expensive contract unless they get a player who produces big-time results? They'll wait until he's cut or becomes a free agent, then pick him up for less. Forget it, I said. If it took eating a player's contract, we would do it. Patrick believed, and he believed on credit, before things started to happen. From that belief the foundation was cast.

> "The graveyards are full of indispensable men."
> —*Charles de Gaulle*

Riles' Rule of Enlightened Self-Interest

The wisest choice a Showtime Warrior can make is to sacrifice superficial self-interest and to underwrite the building of a team that supports his or her skills. You can only receive what you're willing to give.

Great player attitude—with Patrick and Mark Jackson starting and others following—released the Knicks from the confining salary cap and put us four million under cap in just one year! That evolution also meant that some guys are now no longer with the organization. It's a great paradox:

a team player must act out of intense loyalty, even though that loyalty may someday have to be realigned with a new team. *The Winners Within* still try to win, and to cooperate, however, because they know they never lose with that attitude. If you play with total commitment, your present team can win. If you are known as a team player, your chances for a better future are great.

Before day one with the Knicks, I scouted the team's attitude. All the sources said, "They just don't like each other. There's a lot of cliques." The deeper and more important point was that they didn't respect each other. But none of it was out in the open. The season began with the players all nodding their heads. They knew what was expected of them. But they weren't really together. Lip service masked hard-dying old habits.

As the season wore on, the old habits were more alive than dead. Walking into buses, planes, hotel lobbies, restaurants, practice—every group movement became a call to clique-up. Pockets of clique chatter were everywhere: shared negative attitudes, misgivings toward other teammates, justifying this, rationalizing that.

In late January, close to the midseason break, our outstanding performance suddenly fell into a valley.

From the back of the plane en route to a road game versus Golden State I could see I had to act, as I took in an exhibition of cliquing and gesturing, bitching and moaning. Having traveled with pro teams since 1967, I instantly recognized the body language. The looks in their eyes were the Golden Oldies of blame: "It was their fault . . ." "If so-and-so isn't going to do his job . . ."

Coming off the bus from the airport to the hotel,

the players were told to report to a certain room one hour before practice. When they filed in, twelve chairs were waiting in the middle, packed tightly together.

Everyone sat down. I walked in and stood in the back, saying nothing for a long time. They were uncomfortable, looking over their shoulders, wondering what this was all about. Finally, I began. I named the four players who were supposed to be the team's core and said, "I want all four of you to take your chairs and get in the left corner over there."

Then I named the members of another clique. These were the rebels, the players who bitched all the time, who did not respect the voice of their leaders. "All of you take your chairs into the right corner." Three more in another clique were sent into a third corner. Two players who resented not having more playing time were paired up in the fourth corner. One player didn't talk to anybody, and nobody talked to him. I sat him by an empty wall.

They still didn't know what was going on, but the whole reason for this chair-shifting exercise was to define reality. I was holding up a mirror so they could see what they were making of themselves: human islands in a hostile sea, linked only by their gripes. Three here, four there, two over there. . . .

I let three minutes hang in the air. "Okay," I said, "this team has some problems." They looked at me warily, expecting that I would choose somebody's side. They weren't expecting me to put them all on the spot.

"Now, you guys solve the team's problems right now.

"You team leaders—solve the problem by complaining how the other guys reject your leadership, while you don't change and improve your own style of leadership.

"You rebels—solve the problem by ignoring the need for strong leadership. Do what you've been doing. Carry on with your cliquing-in and cliquing-out.

"You other guys—solve the problem by letting everyone else fight among themselves . . . and you, if you guys resent someone playing ahead of you, tell them honestly and openly right now that you think you're better than they are.

"You," I said to the loner. "Take care of our problems by staying isolated, by closing down."

They were fuming. All the subsurface tensions between them were suddenly out in the open. Nobody had a hiding place. Then one of the core players stood up and said, "Don't blame us just because these guys don't listen."

"I'm not talking about blame. Those guys need teaching and we have to do it," I said. "I'm talking about the state the team is in. We can't fix it by placing blame. We are going to fix it when we start pulling together. These divisions show up on the court—in selfishness, in people passing the ball to their clique buddies when another player is open, in failing to work hard for each other. It's crazy. It's taking us right down the tubes!"

We had an hour's discussion about tolerance, openness, and the spirit of understanding. About how losing brings out insecurities, blaming. About sharing the weight.

Things got better after that. The core became stronger, the rebels became more cooperative, the stand-aparts began to take a stake in the team's morale. It took me back to a time ten years earlier, when as a rookie coach I had had to face a team amok with intrateam hatreds and hidden agendas and tell them that a house divided against itself surely could not stand.

Riles' Rule for Surfacing Tension

If you can help people grasp their toxic, destructive behavior in a convincing, physical way, chances are good that they will cut it out and fly right.

We hit another valley, late in the season, and let the Atlantic Division title slip from our hands. Right afterward, we regrouped to play the team's most impressive postseason ball in nineteen years. The way the Knicks picked themselves up again for the playoff run shouted *character*. They took their loss and came back stronger. If we hadn't identified and committed to our core back in January, losing the division title could have just fragmented the team.

Even though the Knicks excelled in 1991–1992, we still occasionally found ways to choke. The difference was that we squeezed each Choke for the maximum of learning and growth. Three quarters of the way through the season, we were seven games ahead of the pack in the Atlantic Division. We had never planned to be there, never discussed it. We just got in shape and played hard, and before we knew it, there we were. We captured the imaginations of a lot of people.

Then we blew it. I let up a little bit instead of driving for one extra win. We lost a couple of late-season games that we could've won, and bang, the division title was gone. While we won ten out of our last sixteen games, which is fair performance, Boston won a phenomenal fifteen of their last sixteen. We ended up tying them, 51–51. Because they had the tie-breaker, they ended up with the division crown and a better seeding position.

We had nobody to blame but ourselves. All season long, big games brought out the Choke in us. We had big leads against strong teams on their courts but couldn't close them out. We saw an image that we desired. We pulled ourselves within reach. We let it get away. Old thought patterns came up, internal voices that said, "You're not the best. You don't deserve the title. The Knicks always go down the tubes at the moment of truth."

Before the playoffs I said to the guys, "You don't even know how damaging this was. When we choked and let this thing get away, we lost what we had worked the whole year to gain. We worked the whole year to gain respect—the respect of the media, of the fans, of your families, of yourself. We lost our credibility as challengers.

"At the end of the year, we were still being characterized as the same Knicks you always were before: a bunch of losers. Heartless, gutless. Could not get the job done."

We let ourselves get mad, then we let ourselves get loose, ready to go after our second chance with free hearts. We held a special pre-playoffs camp in Charleston to find some renewal. I had only one message: "We've got to make them feel our presence." We rekindled the spirit, we had some fun, then we worked hard. It was a good feeling. One night we rented a pool hall. We had hamburgers with chili and beer and staged a tournament. Ev-

"I'm not much of a golfer.
I don't have any friends.
And, all I like to do the day of a game is go home and be alone and worry about ways not to lose."
—"Bear" Bryant

erybody put up twenty bucks, and Patrick Ewing walked away with the money. As if he needs more.

Our playoff challenge: to dump that ingrained fourth-quarter-letdown behavior. That would be our Breakthrough. If we survived Detroit, our second matchup was certain to be Chicago. I thought a little dream of glory might help. I rubbed my hands together, flashed a smile around the locker room, and said, "Guess what, guys? We've got the greatest opportunity in the world. We're the only team that has the chance to beat the two former world champions back-to-back."

Less than a minute and a half into our first Detroit game, the new Knicks announced themselves. It came in the form of a collision between two Warriors, Charles Oakley and Dennis Rodman. A statement was made. Our presence was felt.

> "The first and great commandment is, Don't let them scare you."
> —*Elmer Davis*

The former two-time World Champion Detroit Pistons all of a sudden knew that it was going to be a real series, competitive every inch of the way, against a different Knick team. The credibility and self-esteem we'd lost by blowing the Atlantic Division title we recaptured in one minute and thirteen seconds.

We beat Detroit by thirty in that game. We were on the way to believing in ourselves again. We had made the Breakthrough of becoming a serious contender.

With the Lakers, I'd coached a team with four players who were, in various seasons, all-NBA. It was one of the most talented teams ever brought together.

The challenge wasn't to get their performance level up, it was to keep them consistently at their highest level. The Knicks were a team with less talent. The challenge was to maximize their talents with superb physical conditioning and an awesome work ethic.

Before we went up against the Chicago Bulls in game six of our last playoff series, trailing the series three to two, I told the guys a story about a scorpion and a frog (now familiar to all those who have seen the movie *The Crying Game*). It seems that a frog was about to jump in the frog pond and paddle himself to the other side. Before he plunged in, a scorpion came rustling up next to him and asked a favor. He said, "Take me across on your back."

"Oh, no," the frog said. "You might sting me."

"Why would I do that?" the scorpion said. "If I kill you, I'll die too."

So the frog invited the scorpion to climb on his back, and he started swimming over the water.

Before he got halfway to the other side, he felt a burning jolt at the base of his neck.

"Why did you sting me?" the frog said. "Now we're both going to die!"

"I stung you because that's what I do," the scorpion answered. "I sting frogs. That's my nature."

To drive home the point, I added: "Well . . . we're the New York Knicks. Our culture is very aggressive. We seek to dominate. That's how we play.

- Our culture is hardworking.
- Our philosophy is defense-focused.
- Our defense is aggressive.
- Our aggressiveness is domination-driven.

"That's who we are. That's how we play. It's our nature. We sting Bulls.

"And there's one more thing. Sometime this

summer," I then told the team, "some shoe company's marketing executives will hold a conference. I'm wondering if any of you will be there."

One player looked up with a puzzled expression. "You *might* be there," I continued, looking first at him, and then caught each of the other eleven pairs of eyes, "in the form of a photograph. Every game the Bulls play, photographers wait for Michael Jordan to come hard to the hole, flying in with the ball over his head, tongue hanging out, eyes riveted on the rim, going for a monster dunk.

"Now, somebody's always underneath Michael in these pictures. They might be bent back, getting out of his way, or they might be standing flat-footed, totally faked out. The marketing experts will review dozens of photos. They'll pick the best one, slap it on a poster, and print eight million copies."

The players instantly got what I was driving at.

"If your photo comes out real nice, if Michael looks like a god while you look like you don't even belong in the same gym, then you could be Michael Jordan's newest poster boy."

The body language of the whole team changed. Their shoulder muscles tensed. Guys who had been leaning forward drew upright in their seats, pressing the floor with the balls of their feet.

"One thing a New York Knick will not be is anybody's poster boy, even if the camera makes us look like one. We ain't one. It's an attitude more than anything." I asked, looking right into their eyes: "Who wants to be the guy that's going to open up the lane? Who wants to make it *convenient* for some superstar to kick your ass? Because if that's how you're going to play, you should leave right now."

> ### Riles' Rule of Respect
> Sometimes you have to respect your competition so much that you treat them with no respect at all. You have to defeat a great player's aura more than his game.

Muhammad Ali was a seven-to-one underdog against a proven, durable champion named Sonny Liston. He respected Liston's strength, but he respected himself even more. Joe Namath showed no respect for Johnny Unitas and the Baltimore Colts when he said the Jets would whip them in Super Bowl III.

Everybody else in the world expected the solid, seasoned Colts to win. Namath and the rest of the Jets whipped the Colts, 16–7. Would Bill Gates and Microsoft have made fortunes had they bowed and scraped to IBM instead of feeding Big Blue a knuckle sandwich? Could Phil Knight have made Nike the most powerful firm in sports marketing if he had respected the Converse Chuck Taylor All-Star sneaker as the ultimate in basketball court footwear?

To have any chance of rising, the Knicks had to go beyond their respect for Jordan, a man who is unquestionably the greatest basketball player of the day. They had to focus themselves on gaining respect from Jordan himself. Jordan is uniquely gifted. He plays hard. He wants to win. He has all the skills. We'd love to have him on our team, any time. But that's not the hand we were dealt. Our job is to beat him when he's armed with his best weapons.

And his subtlest weapon of all is his mastery at

gamesmanship, at outpsyching the opponents. Players revere him so much, they become deferential.

"Jordan will tear your heart out and splatter it on the floor," I said. "And he will do it with a smile. But he will always come to the basket with a will to win."

Whenever a Chicago Bull went to the basket, intending to throw down a dunk that would rock the stadium, we would come to stop him—just as hard as he had come to score. Whenever he showed us how much he wanted to win, we had to show him that we wanted the same thing, just as much. We simply didn't want to defer. Without that attitude we'd be handing the Bulls a license to tear our hearts out for the next several years.

The Knicks' performance in game six shut down the Bulls' offense for more than six minutes of the final quarter. Patrick Ewing, with a badly sprained ankle, threw down twenty-seven points. We stung the Bulls by a 100–86 score, and we did it in the crucial final period, the part of the game that had been our Achilles' heel all year long. The Bulls may not have respected our style. But they certainly came to respect our will to win.

Before round two of the 1992 playoffs, the *New York Post* had run an all-caps headline: KNICKS BEST HOPE: LOOK GOOD LOSING.

Over the six games, we surprised everyone that we had gotten so far. The Bulls' whining over our playing style and subsequent media attention to a sixth-game foul set the tone for game seven. Prior to game seven, I gave a lot of thought to the stacked deck we faced. It would have meant a huge fine, but I wanted to put myself on record:

"There's no chance we can win game seven. The sponsors, the fans, the press love the drama and exposure. Now, though, they don't want the lowly New York Knicks to beat the marquee-value World Champion Chicago Bulls in game seven."

I didn't mean the game was going to be fixed, or that it was truly impossible for us to win. I meant that several powerful forces would be pulling, even if unconsciously, for a Bulls' victory. We hadn't yet planted a seed in everyone's psyche that we were legitimate, that we deserved to end up on top. There were nagging voices even within our own minds, suspicions that our bubble *had* to burst. Somehow or other the collective force of that unconscious will would come out. Something would change the flow of the game. I knew this because I had worked for a decade with the player who had reigned in the "greatest-ever" throne just before Michael Jordan. I knew what breaks Earvin Johnson would get in a seventh game. I knew that Michael Jordan would, in his turn, end up getting sympathetic treatment from the officials in some form or another. It's just human nature. Sport is a dramatic spectacle. Ultimately, everybody wants the guy in the white hat to win.

Riles' Rule of the Stacked Deck

When you're playing against a stacked deck, compete even harder. Show the world how much you'll fight for the winner's circle. If you do, someday the cellophane will crackle off a fresh pack, one that belongs to you, and the cards will be stacked in your favor.

Not long after the Knicks' game-six win, I made a game-seven prediction to Dave Checketts: "Jordan will collect ten free throws in the first period. And they'll suddenly put Patrick Ewing on the bench—with a third foul early in the second period or else a fourth foul early in the third period."

I was close enough: Jordan got eight. We couldn't put a hand on him. Every time he put the ball on the floor and we touched him, however slightly, the officials sent him to the line. Every time I questioned the officials, they told me to shut up. Patrick had only one foul in the entire first half. By early in the third quarter we were only three points back, with a chance at one of the great upsets in playoff history. Suddenly, in the space of one minute and thirty-five seconds, Patrick drew three consecutive calls. Four minutes into the period, he had to ride the bench. When the quarter ended, we were down by eighteen.

Game and series lost.

Jordan drew more than fouls. He drew star treatment. Either consciously or unconsciously, the officials tailored game seven to his style of play.

We lost, but we had extended the Bulls, on their way to a back-to-back championship, more convincingly than any other team in the league.

We reminded a championship team—and Chicago truly was one—that they had to take on all comers and all styles. And they did. We paid our dues. The upstart always has to overcome more, just as a start-up business has to struggle with so many more challenges than an established one. Upstarts don't win championships unless they score an absolute knockout. Upstarts win the right to come back next time and *compete* for the championship. That right is the key.

The Winner Within's Ladder of Evolution

- From nobody to *UPSTART*
- From upstart to *CONTENDER*
- From contender to *WINNER*
- From winner to *CHAMPION*
- From champion to *DYNASTY*

For 1991–1992, the Knicks' Mastery was in the grass roots, the simple values of what it took to be successful. We got behind one voice. We defined ourselves as a kind of family, shunning leaks, backstabbing, and negative press stories. The Knicks aimed for a conceptual goal, a solid, value-oriented base. For us, it was Hard Work, Conditioning, and Professionalism. From that philosophy, the specifics flowed. The 1992 New York Knicks pulled themselves through years' worth of phases and stages in one single season. That's incredibly fast. And set the stage for even greater excellence in the year that followed.

Dr. Lew Richfield epitomizes the "movin' on" attitude: "I'm excited every morning," he beams. "I want to know what's going to walk into my office today. What kind of hand-to-hand combat I'm going to face. We must have that. It's very important to have new goals all the time." Beatrice Wood is a famous ceramic artist who just celebrated her 100th birthday. Over lunch once, Lew asked her, "What gets you up each day?" and she said, "I just have to see what's in the kiln every morning."

Time-Out

After Core Cracking has created its inevitable ruins, there is only one real alternative for *The Winner Within,* and that is Moving On. It is to search out new teams, goals, and challenges—either in the same place or in a new setting. Properly understood, Moving On is not a retreat from defeat, but an exhilarating change that makes you feel vital and alive. Armed with an awareness of the total cycle of team success, the next adventure can only—after all—be that much richer and so much easier to manage. And the first triumph after Moving On is to become an upstart who quickly earns the right to compete for a championship and who takes the bold first steps of a totally Innocent Climb.

12

One from the Heart

"Death is afraid of him because he has the heart of a lion."
—*Arab proverb*

Y ou don't win a game all at once. A basketball game is an event-filled forty-eight-minute stream of possessions—shots, blocks, rebounds, steals, passes, fast breaks—just as a year in the life of a family or a business is a 365-day-a-year event stream. It isn't humanly possible to win on every possession, to score every time you get the ball, or to block your opponent's shot every time the ball is in their hands.

No matter what your sport or your role in life, there are always smaller encounters within the larger whole. There are skirmishes within a battle, battles within a campaign, and campaigns within a war. Each small victory improves the odds that you will triumph at the moment of truth. So *The Winner Within* strives to win on every possession, collecting the small victories and building to the

big ones; and that is what this chapter is about: the
victories I have seen in my life, both large and
small, a significant parade of winners who play the
game of life at the highest level.

Riles' Rule of the Magic Moment

In every contest, there comes a moment that defines
winning from losing. The true Warrior understands
and seizes that moment by giving an effort so intensive and so intuitive that it could only be called one
from the heart.

The first person in my winners' parade is very
familiar to you. That person of course is Earvin
Johnson.

From my sidelines post at hundreds of games, I
could sense when Earvin decided that it was time
for the moment of truth to unfold. It could have
been during a meaningless practice scrimmage—
or the closing seconds of a year-long championship
drive—whatever the stakes, his sudden and confident shift of behavior would announce the defining moment: this is the time to ice the win.

The ball is inbounded to him. He knows exactly
what he has to do and he begins to orchestrate,
waving his teammates to certain areas on the
court. He dribbles out to the wing and begins to
back his defender in, watching all the players, sizing up the overall defense, comparing the game
clock and the shot clock, knowing precisely when
to make his move.

Somewhere in the tempo of his dribble, Earvin
hears an inner clock chiming. It tells him the time
is now: he switches the dribble to his left hand, lifts
his big shoulders, and turns his head toward the

"You've got to sing
Like you don't need
the money.
You've got to love
Like you'll never get
hurt.
You've got to dance
Like there's nobody
watching.
You've got to come
from the heart
If you want it to
work."
—Susanna Clark

baseline. The defender reacts by shifting his weight toward the baseline, just as Earvin lowers his shoulders and spins around in a completely opposite direction, slicing into the lane and drawing two more defenders—a center and a power forward. As they converge in his path, Earvin begins a hook shot. The defenders jump with their arms stretched to form a human fence ten feet tall. Earvin keeps his eye on the rim, brings the ball, head high, in a predictable arc, then suddenly changes the angle of his wrist and, with his fingertips, snaps a pass to a Laker who is approaching from the opposite baseline. That player grabs the pass and jams it through the hoop, totally untouched by defenders. And that's the play that puts the game out of reach.

A trademark of the true Warrior, a Showtime Warrior, is that inner clock . . . and an overarching view of all the games within the big game. The true Warrior is someone who knows how to get the job done at the moment of truth.

Of all the competitors I've known in a thirty-five-year-plus sports and sports-business career, Earvin stands out as the purest example of a Warrior. I can picture his face captured by Edward Curtis in a sepia-toned photograph. I can see him in the trappings of a Native American leader, because the same tremendous pride and dignity shines through from inside. He would look perfectly natural wearing war paint, buckskin, and a headdress of eagle feathers: a study in HEART, COURAGE and WILL . . . for it is these three traits that define a Showtime Warrior, be it an Earvin Johnson or a Patrick Ewing.

> ### Riles' Rule of the Warrior
> The Warrior is an immortal vision of what all *Winners Within* aspire to be. That one person who makes a difference to any significant team.

"Give what you have. To someone, it may be better than you dare to think."
—*Longfellow*

Earvin didn't just make a difference to his team, he transformed the entire NBA as an institution as well. About three years ago the Lakers were desperate to sign an outside shooter, but salary-cap restrictions stood in the way. Earvin Johnson stepped into the picture and voluntarily gave back several hundred thousand dollars of his pay to make the deal possible.

Nobody in the league had ever heard of such a thing happening before. Now it happens every year.

Early in the 1991–1992 season, several New York Knicks players—including Mark Jackson and Patrick Ewing—allowed their contracts to be renegotiated so the team could add new people. Charles Barkley, who comes off in the media as the most self-centered superstar in the league, recently handed back a chunk of salary to his new team, the Phoenix Suns, to help them bring aboard the outside shooting threat of Danny Ainge. His teammate, Tom Chambers, did the same. Like everyone else in the NBA, these guys were simply learning from Earvin. It's no coincidence that both the Suns and the Knicks had the best records in their conference in 1993, and jockeyed to compete for the ultimate prize. Earvin's example led them.

To scale these heights demands something far stronger than aggressive spirit. To be *the one per-*

son who makes a difference within a significant team, you have to have love—for yourself, for those who work alongside of you, for the potentials inside the game itself. To be a Showtime Warrior, you always have to be ready to give one from the heart.

For a true Warrior, love is more than just a sentiment. It's an attitude that leads to success.

Putting your team first isn't really sacrifice. This attitude hasn't made Earvin poor. Not only does he own memories and career satisfactions beyond what most of us can imagine, he's also a millionaire many times over.

Now it's making him a different kind of Most Valuable Player, in the fight against AIDS.

Instead of getting caught up in remorse or self-pity over his own situation, he's learned and he's grown from the experience. Even though his basketball days are over and the extent of his life-span is unknowable, Earvin is still out there expressing his vitality, serving, making a contribution, helping humanity cope with its modern-day equivalent of the plague.

"Being on the tightrope is living; everything else is waiting."
—*Karl Wallenda*

I was rocked by the news when Earvin announced to the world on November 7th, 1991, that he had tested positive for Human Immunodeficiency Virus.

On that day, I was preparing the Knicks for a home-court meeting with the Orlando Magic. Phone messages from Earvin's manager kept trailing me all day, but it wasn't until practice was over that I had time to find out why he had been calling. The news left me speechless. I had to hang up, pull myself together, and call back a moment later. I was ready to drop all my responsibilities and fly out to Los Angeles immediately, until he convinced me that the world didn't have to stop. The right thing was to stay where I was and do what I do best.

That night, just prior to the scheduled tipoff, I addressed the Madison Square Garden fans. My words stumbled at times, but they got rescued by the kind of eloquence that comes from speaking from the heart. "I would like all of us . . . if we could . . ." I began searchingly. "Obviously, there was some very bad news today for all of us who support professional basketball and are Earvin Magic Johnson fans.

"It's very important for us right now at this time—in your own voice, in your own beliefs, in any way you desire—to take a moment of silence. To give our love and our support and our prayers for Earvin, for his family, for the one million people who are infected with an insidious disease that needs our understanding. I know the New York Knicks family, organization, players would like to recite our own prayer. And that power will go along to helping Earvin recover."

With that, all the players from both teams came together at center court and placed their hands in the middle of a circle, becoming a single team with a single purpose. We said The Lord's Prayer together. Then the game began, and life went on.

The best leaders are often the best listeners and the most open to new ideas. When Earvin made the transition from basketball player to AIDS fighter, he realized that he had plenty to learn, and he's managed to put his own situation to the side so well and studied the issues so well that he's probably the most effective spokesperson in the AIDS war today.

"You can become a winner only if you are willing to walk over the edge."
—*Damon Runyon*

The world of basketball has no monopoly on Show-time Warriors. At the 1992 Barcelona Olympics, Chris and I witnessed a remarkable athletic moment which also flashed heart, courage, and will in abundance, a triumph which made a difference to an entire nation.

Arriving in Barcelona was like splashing down into a sea of national pride. Flags draped everywhere. Immaculate streets and smiling Spaniards no matter where you went. It was impossible not to feel the spirit.

To at least one Spaniard, a runner named Fermin Cacho, that spirit made all the difference. In Montjuic Stadium on the last day of Olympic competition, the men's 1500-meter race was billed as a tough battle between an Algerian named Nouredine Morceli and two runners from Kenya—Joe Cheshire and David Kibet. The Kenyans took off quickly out of the blocks. When Morceli drew near, one stayed in front of him, hugging the inside of the track, and one pulled up alongside his outside shoulder. They had him pinned in a box, forced to run the race at their tempo. Their strategy was to keep the race slow, then gamble on winning it with a strong finishing kick.

Cacho was not considered a contender in the event, but the mostly-Spanish crowd kept their eyes on him all the way as he kept pace behind the three leaders. They were thrilled that he could remain so close. Suddenly, with only two hundred meters left, approaching the final turn, Morceli slid four lines wide to escape the Kenyans' trap. Cheshire edged outward slightly to block his path. That created a brief opening on the inside, and Cacho shot through.

Suddenly he found himself in the lead, with the Kenyans now on his heels. The crowd went wild.

I swung my binoculars toward King Juan Carlos and Queen Sofia. They were standing with their hands clasped in front of their hearts. Thirty meters ahead of the finish line, Cacho passed in front of the Royal Box. He lifted a wave to his King and Queen, then finished his sprint.

One hundred twenty-five thousand emotional spectators leaped to their feet. Cacho slowed to a jog and slipped a Spanish flag over his shoulders for his victory lap. It was a magnificent moment. He had run for his King and for his country. They were the wings for his feet, and his feet had triumphed for his nation.

"Presume not that I am the thing I was."
—*William Shakespeare*

But what happens to an athlete once the legs stop running? Is there a life after the arena for the Showtime Warrior?

Literally thousands of once-outstanding pro and college athletes crash and burn when it comes to creating victories in their life beyond the playing field. It's a mystery and an irony. People who are revered from the time they star on their junior high school's team to the time they're bigshots on a college campus and then hot tickets in a pro league are also people who reach the middle years of their life unprepared. All of a sudden, the support and adulation they'd been used to, and felt naturally entitled to, stops cold. Some settle into obscure, marginal careers. Some hit bottom. Until recently, an ex-Laker's back-to-back NBA championship ring was on display in a Beverly Hills pawnshop. Not long ago, a former Rams fullback, still relatively young, died on skid row.

Dave Bing is a different story. Bing came to the

Detroit Pistons as the first player taken in the 1966 draft. He was the tenth-best scorer in the league as a rookie and won the 1967 Rookie of the Year award. By his second year he was the leading scorer in the league, averaging over twenty-seven points a game. He eventually made First Team All-NBA twice and was voted MVP of the All-Star Game in 1976. He's now on the very select list of NBA All-Time Greats.

Before that, Dave Bing went to Syracuse University, where advisers said he should skip the serious courses that might interfere with his concentration on basketball. Since he came from a poor Washington, D.C., neighborhood, they figured him for a classroom dud. He didn't buy into their thinking. And he continued his education, even during his pro years, reading hundreds of books on road trips, hustling off-season jobs at a bank, at Chrysler, and at a steel company. Educating himself, basically, in the skills of business.

"To be prepared is half the victory."
—*Miguel Cervantes*

Today Bing is CEO of three different multimillion-dollar companies: a steel plant, a metal stamping company, and a construction company. Over three hundred people are on his payroll. He's not only one of the most successful black businessmen in the country, he's also a serious prospect for the mayor's office.

One finds Showtime Warriors in every walk of life:

A few years ago Walt Disney Company CEO Michael Eisner called me and invited me to speak to a group of Walt Disney animators because of the key role these talented people would play in the next era of Disney success. It was not long after Michael had joined the company. This was just as the Disney animators were on the verge of a whole new wave of classics, such as *The Little Mermaid, Beauty and the Beast* and *Aladdin*.

Eisner is a sports-loving guy and a true Showtime Warrior. He calls himself and his group of managers and co-executives "Team Disney." What did Eisner bring to Disney? Like many teams in business, the animators needed a good cheerleader to help them rejuvenate and reinvent the team, so Eisner took the quality people that were already there, added a few draft choices, and created a new enthusiasm.

Basically, they inundated the team with one concept: excellence at everything you do. Team Disney is closer than many athletic squads. They know each other's moves. They work almost entirely on body language. Eye contact. Sentence fragments. I can imagine Michael gesturing and nodding just like Earvin when he orchestrates a downcourt campaign. And the fast-paced enthusiasm works. The boom times for Disney—animation and the rest of their businesses—haven't stopped yet.

■　■　■

Some Showtime Warriors in business earn their war bonnet for taking a stand on values. At a speaking engagement last summer I got to know Ted Forstmann, a financier who took a stand during the two-year peak of the 1980s junk bond frenzy. Knowing that the prevailing thinking on Wall Street was out of whack, he stayed away and didn't make a single deal. Instead, he sat on close to three billion dollars of available money.

When the junk bond market collapsed in 1989, Forstmann's company stood almost alone as the only firm still strong enough to make significant buyout deals. In an impassioned editorial for *The Wall Street Journal,* he wrote that the problem wasn't so much the crooked guys—there would always be crooked guys. The problem was in how many decent, substantial people had been so seduced into siding with the fast buck. "You had all these little yuppie guys running around, calculating this and that, creating securities that would never be paid off," Forstmann explained to me. "I just got concerned that America might not make it."

What Forstmann teaches *The Winner Within* is the *power of restraint.* He bided his time until the right values returned to earn a just reward for his stakeholders in the style of a true champion. He stood back and refused to let the fear of being wrong intimidate him.

> "One man with courage makes a majority."
> —*Andrew Jackson.*

Literature and the arts have their Showtime Warriors, too. David Halberstam is an outstanding example. Recently, Halberstam explained to me his relentless determination to excel that is so much a part of the Showtime Warrior. He told me about his own triumphant war against complacency.

Some years ago Halberstam had written a successful, critically acclaimed book covering Bobby Kennedy's final campaign. Another author also wrote a book on the same topic which was no greater a commercial success. But when Halberstam read his rival's book, it was plain that the other author had worked harder, had done more research. That left Halberstam deeply embarrassed, and he vowed that it was the last time any other writer would outwork him.

And his very next book, *The Best and the Brightest,* was not only a bestseller, it was one of the most significant books of its decade. Since then, Halberstam has written an unbroken string of bestsellers. He demands that every book he puts his name to withstand measurement against his own Showtime Warrior standard.

Not every winner gets treated to the same notoriety that a CEO or a star athlete or celebrity enjoys. Fortunately for the rest of us, there are thousands of great team players throughout society. They're recognized only once in a while, which means that such a person is all the more worth studying when he or she does get noticed.

Riles' Rule of Recognition

The less reason for an everyday person to be recognized, the more reason to pay attention to the recognition. It takes true greatness for a noncelebrity to capture the heartbeat of public admiration. But just remember, money, position, power, and recognition are residual rewards of winning.

My familiarity with the American Teacher Awards, coincidentally awarded by the Walt Disney Company, is long-standing. I presented the first sports teacher's award to Morgan Wooten—a terrific coach in Washington, D.C., and a true "lifer"—who has been doing the same job superbly for decades. Rafe Esquith made headlines recently for winning the highest American Teacher Award. Before that, he was barely known outside a crowded grade school in the middle of a riot-damaged Los Angeles neighborhood.

Hobart Elementary sits in Koreatown, surrounded by a half-burned-out commercial strip.

Right now, L.A.'s schools are in terrible budget turmoil, making double-digit cuts in teacher pay, trying to ward off a strike. Rafe Esquith holds down two part-time jobs on the side so he'll have money for taking his thirty-six students on field trips. He hits campus before sunrise and stays way after sundown. Every year, his kids present a Shakespearean play. They also walk away annually with the districtwide mathematics competition.

Most of those kids are poor. Many are immigrants, living in homes where no English is spoken. No place does America need leaders more than in the classrooms of youngsters like these.

One of them, Michelle Ibanez, knows the uplift of the Esquith schoolroom: "Every day when I get up and look out the window and think about my world," she said, "it seems hopeless. Then I come to this class and I feel like maybe anything is possible." The Showtime Warrior reignites our belief that anything *is* possible.

Like Rafe Esquith, Elizabeth Glaser sparks that conviction, too. Elizabeth has led the way in helping children with AIDS (she stands about as tall as Earvin Johnson's rib cage, but she has become Earvin's mentor in the battle against this dreaded disease).

Elizabeth Glaser is the wife of Paul Glaser, a television director who once starred in the "Starsky and Hutch" TV series. In August of 1981, after a difficult pregnancy that ended with the cesarean birth of their daughter, Ariel, she received a massive blood transfusion—seven pints. Three weeks later, reading a newspaper story, she learned for the first time about a deadly, newly emerging virus called HIV (blood banks weren't screening for HIV until early 1985). By that time, Ariel had already become ill. Elizabeth had gotten the virus from her transfusion, had passed it on to Ariel through breast-feeding, and then subsequently on to their young son, Jake. At first, the diagnosis made her want to fall apart. Then it made her take action.

Ariel Glaser lived three years beyond the detection of her illness. By then, Elizabeth had already taken on the fight against AIDS in children as her full-time concern. She established the Pediatric AIDS Foundation and launched the Ariel Project, which is about preventing mother-to-child HIV transmission. Along the way, she wrote an extremely moving book, *In the Absence of Angels.*

Motivation can't come from anyplace deeper in the heart than the urge to protect children. But Elizabeth Glaser linked her motivation to courage. She forged urgency out of tragedy and action out of disaster.

A person can rise to Warrior stature from almost any starting point, no matter how unlikely, using almost any kind of talent or ability. A couple of years ago, the *Los Angeles Times* started running some unusual cartoons in their Sunday magazine. They were single-panel drawings that looked like they came out of a sixth-grader's notebook: edgy, clever, satirical, maybe even tasteless, nearly always touching on topics that provoke nervousness. They were signed in a scrawl: JOHN CALLAHAN.

John Callahan's life is the kind that makes people hard-bitten. His mother abandoned him. He was adopted by an Oregon couple who thought they were infertile, but subsequently had several kids of their own. Callahan felt like an outsider in

> "Morale is the state of mind. It is steadfastness and courage and hope."
> —*General George Marshall*

his own family, so he developed a wicked sense of humor as his defense.

Another defense he developed was wiping out his bitter feelings with alcohol. One night shortly after his twenty-first birthday, after drinking an inordinate amount of beer, he handed the keys to his Volkswagen Bug to a drinking buddy. They went speeding out onto a freeway south of L.A.

The next thing Callahan knew, his VW was wrapped around a billboard, collapsed by a ninety-mile-per-hour impact. The crash severed his spine. He could scarcely use his hands. The drinking buddy got out okay and was never heard from again.

Months and years of alcoholism and self-pity went by. One night he spent a solid hour trying to open a bottle with his teeth. It slipped out of his grip, then rolled across the floor, out of reach. He stared at it awhile. Then he started yelling at it. Then he started cursing God for the crippled state of his body. He yelled until he was exhausted, then he burst into tears and cried for an hour.

Finally, an eerie but comforting sensation came over him, as if a hand were soothing him. When his attendant got back, Callahan said, "Hey, Alex, something really profound happened to me here. I don't think I'm gonna drink anymore."

From that night on, Callahan began achieving things, using his heart and his courage. He checked into AA and achieved sobriety. He developed an outlet for his humor, clutching a pen in his right hand and guiding it with his left. He found people who believed in his talent and helped get it out into the world.

Callahan's humor has a savage quality. It offends some people, but lots of others—especially

> "You need to play with supreme confidence, or else you'll lose again, and then losing becomes a habit."
> —*Joe Paterno*

among the 43 million Americans who are classified as handicapped—find that something liberating happens when you laugh about adversities. One of his extended pieces is even called "The Lighter Side of Being Paralyzed for Life." He'd rather turn painful situations into jokes than be indulged by a pitying, patronizing attitude.

One drawing shows two beggars on a city street corner. Each has lost his entire torso and is reduced to nothing but a head on a wheeled platform, with a tin cup. Worse yet, the man on the left is wearing dark glasses, evidently blind. The other man looks his way and says, "People like you are an inspiration to me."

In spite of poking fun at the idea, Callahan can't escape the fact that he actually is an inspiration—on his own terms. He inspires a belief in endurance and resilience. In fact, his life is now being adapted into a Robin Williams movie. Callahan put the brakes on all the things that used to be eating him. He can enjoy a healthy self-respect. He can help the rest of us laugh at stuff that scares us. That qualifies him as a Showtime Warrior.

Riles' Rule of Will

Each Warrior wants to leave the mark of his will, his signature, on important acts he touches. This is not the voice of ego but of the human spirit, rising up and declaring that it has something to contribute to the solution of the hardest problems, no matter how vexing!

It isn't enough just to play the game—the Showtime Warrior wants to leave the mark of his will on the game itself.

Rafe Esquith showed it by providing immigrant kids in a hard-hit neighborhood a better education than they might get at a high-priced private school. Elizabeth Glaser showed it by digging in against an insidious illness that took away her daughter and by helping other people avoid the same heartbreak. Earvin Johnson shows it today every time he steps forward and speaks out in the war to whip AIDS.

As I write this, I sense that the last link of the winner's cycle is locking into place. Why is the face of Earvin Johnson so much both the face of the Showtime Warrior and the face of the Innocent Climber as well?

We have come so far from our starting point. We have endured and understood so many tests to advance through the cycle of winning . . . and yet we appear to be no further ahead for it all.

Or are we?

Wordsworth penned a great truth when he said that "The child is father of the man."

Maybe what we really want from life is simply to possess *knowing innocence*. But we can only achieve it by scaling this ascent:

> "I am a Shawnee. My forefathers were warriors. Their son is a warrior . . . From my tribe I take nothing. I am the maker of my own fortune."
> —*Tecumseh*

The INNOCENT CLIMB is the first rustling of our proper selves.

The DISEASE OF ME stages the most primitive assault on our own goodness.

The CORE COVENANT is a conscious fresh start through commitment to others.

THUNDERBOLTS test our conviction and our determination to stay the course.

THE CHOKE reveals our deepest-seated anxieties about being a winner.

BREAKTHROUGHS enable us to conquer our own self-devised handicaps.

COMPLACENCY deludes us to believe that we can ever do enough.

MASTERY teaches us that we must always do more.

ANTEING UP turns Mastery into unbeatable excellence.

Until the Covenant's exhausted CORE CRACKS.

And, one must MOVE ON mentally—and perhaps physically, too—to a new rebirth.

It all has the rhythm of breathing . . . of the expanding-contracting world of growth.

Through my second year with the Knicks we've strived to bring the team through its evolutionary phases as quickly as possible, with our eyes on the ultimate prize—becoming a truly significant team. Much of the time, as I've hustled through airport lobbies to catch flights and as I've kicked back in hotel rooms waiting for game time to roll around once more, there's been a certain book in my hands. It's a volume of selected wisdom from the long, incredible career of the late folklorist/mythologist/teacher Joseph Campbell: *Reflections on the Art of Living*.

A good friend of ours, a *Winner Within* herself, Barbara Barry, gifted me with this book.

It's deep, heady stuff, full of pearls. One phrase in particular runs through my mind as this book comes to its inevitable close. Ten simple words: "The privilege of a lifetime is being who you are."

I only have this to add. I know who you are. You are *The Winner Within*. The book you've just read is just an attempt to lay out a road map showing how to get from wherever you are now all the way up to where you belong. You have everything it takes to lift your team and yourself to great, long-lasting achievements, to fulfillment of potential. To a lifetime of significance.

Go for it.

Every now and then, somewhere, some place, sometime, you are going to have to plant your feet, stand firm, and make a point about who you are and what you believe in.

When that time comes, Pat, you simply have to do it.

—Lee Riley